LUCINDA O'

# Little Black Book of
# Great Places to Stay

# IRELAND

### Enchanting Houses,
### Castles, Hotels and Spas

TSAR PRESS

This book is published by

TSAR PRESS

Post Office Box No.9647
Glenageary, Co. Dublin

www.lucindaosullivan.com
www.wheretostayinireland.com

Publishing Editor Brendan O'Sullivan
Written By Lucinda O'Sullivan

Regional Editor Margaret Browne
Maps and mapping: Joe Morris
Technical Support: Ian McDonnell O'Sullivan
Layout: Susan waine, Ashfield Press
Web: Peter Sutton Fitzgibbon - webpagedesignco.com

ISBN 0-9547256-0-3

Printed in Ireland by
ColourBooks Ltd

# a word from Lucinda

Irish people are flying all over Europe, nay the World, at the moment on great value tickets to see great value places. Grand, if that's what one wants. However, I have roasted beside pools in every country in Europe, I have drunk the Sangria and the Ouzo, sipped the Riesling and White Port, but I have never in any of these countries had the craic that you can have around Ireland, and I have kissed the tarmac at Dublin Airport every time I have come home.

Many of you may feel the same, or want to combine a bit of both, for this book has come about by virtue of all the letters and emails I have received over the years as Restaurant/Food Critic with The Sunday Independent. Scores of you have said "you wrote about a place two years ago, but we can't remember the name, could you please compile a book and website of lovely places where we can go and spend our money."

Travelling the Country, I have stayed in some wonderful establishments and met some wonderful hosts but, on the downside, I have also had miserable nights in thin beds with non to clean floors and bedlinen, hand wringing landladies and shirking hosts, skimpy breakfasts, with thimbles of watery orange juice, so this book is to save you from those perils.

The Country and City Houses, Castles, special Hotels, and Spas in My Little Black Book are rich in their thinking and attitude towards the guest and the tourists. Some are lavish and luxurious, some are simple and sincere, some are creative and humorous, but here you can expect, at all different levels, the finest of what Ireland has to offer by way of hospitality, friendship, helpfulness and value for money.

Don't forget to use the website www.lucindaosullivan.com which will be updated throughout the year.

Get out there and enjoy.

# ireland

Ireland, perceived as the Emerald Isle, Land of the Shamrock, the Leprechaun, the Blarney Stone, Thatched and White Washed Cottages, and the attitude of "as God made time he made plenty of it" has changed dramatically in recent years. It is now a thriving progressive country holding its head high as a member of the European Union but City traffic is bumper to bumper from early morning as workers head for their places of employment to keep the wheels of progress turning. However, underneath all the hustle and bustle, people haven't changed all that much. They still like to meet and talk, share a story, have a laugh and generally enjoy life.

Sport is an intrinsic interest with the major equestrian industry being in showjumping and horse racing. Our golf courses are a match for any in the World and our golfers, of the standing of Padraig Harrington, Darren Clarke, Paul McGinley, regularly contest major competitions world wide. Rugby and soccer both have a solid following but the major football game is Gaelic football with interest reaching its climax at the end of September when the all Ireland Final between the two leading Counties is played. For visitors possibly the most fascinating sport is traditional hurling, which is probably the fastest field game in the world, requiring speed, fitness, physical strength, great skill and application.

The open countryside, from the pleasant valleys and rounded mountains of the East to the rugged features of the West, provide ample scope and pleasant diversity of scenery for the walker or cyclist. For the motorist there are limitless places of interest from ancient ruins, fine buildings and museums, breathtaking scenery and even a Fairy Tree on the Comeragh drive near Dungarvan. The gourmet is well catered for as each and every county provides some excellent Restaurants to please even the most demanding palate.

Most pubs and bars provide good value lunches during the day and, in the evenings, many of them have traditional musicians and singers and, as we say in Ireland, the craic.

Most of all, apart from the sport, scenery, food, drink, craic, music the main attraction must be the people themselves, generally warm friendly and welcoming.

Ireland – you won't be disappointed.

# explanation of symbols

The symbols are a guide to facilities rather than a positive statement, and may change, so check important points when booking.

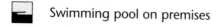 Working Farm

Children welcome, no age limits, but cots, high chairs etc are not necessarily available.

Credit Cards accepted – generally Visa/MC

T.V. in bedrooms

Swimming pool on premises

P  Parking

Wine Licence – Hotels have full licences.

Disabled Facilities – check level with establishment.

Non-Smoking House

Pets welcome but may have to sleep in outbuilding or car. Check.

Pets accommodated in house.

Bikes on loan or for hire.

Tennis Court on premises

# contents

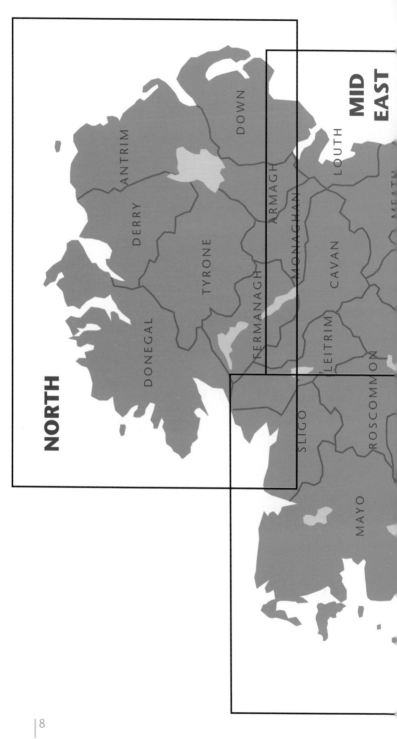

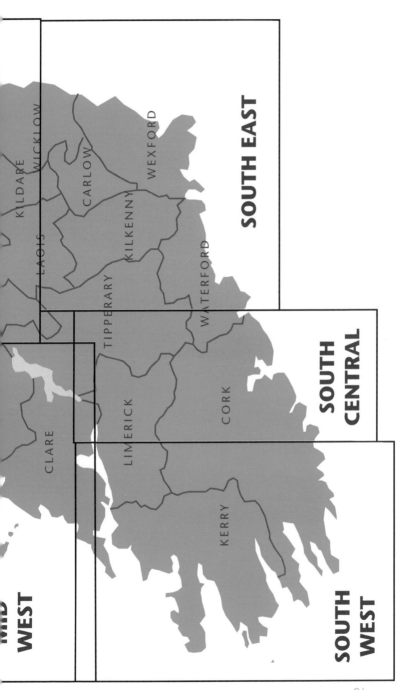

KILDARE

WICKLOW

CARLOW

WEXFORD

LAOIS

KILKENNY

TIPPERARY

WATERFORD

CLARE

LIMERICK

CORK

KERRY

SOUTH EAST

SOUTH
CENTRAL

SOUTH
WEST

MID
WEST

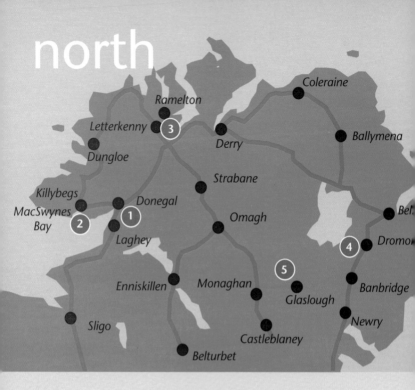

1. Coxtown Manor
2. CastleMurray House Hotel
3. Frewin
4. Clanmurry
5. Castle Leslie

1. Drummond Mews
2. Aberdeen Lodge
3. Merrion Hall
4. Cedar Lodge
5. Browne's Hotel & Restaurant
6. Portmarnock Hotel & Golf Links
7. Redbank house & Restaurant
8. Viewmount House

# south-east

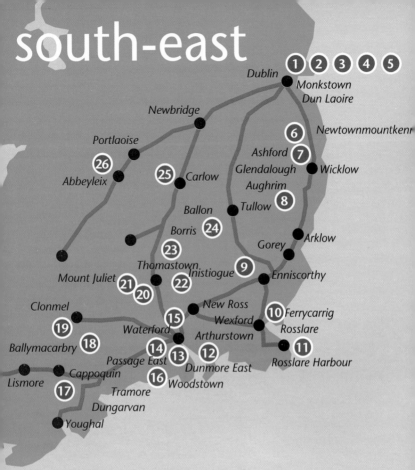

1. Brownes Hotel
2. Aberdeen Lodge
3. Merrion Hall
4. Cedar Lodge
5. Drummond Mews
6. Druids Glen
7. Ballyknocken House
8. Clone House
9. Monfin House
10. Ferrycarrig Hotel
11. Kelly's Resort Hotel
12. Glendine Country House
13. Foxmount Country House
14. Waterford Castle
15. Sion Hill House & Gdns
16. Gaultier Lodge
17. Richmond House
18. Glasha Country House
19. Kilmaneen Farmhouse
20. Belmore
21. Mount Juliet
22. Cullintra House
23. The Step House
24. Sherwood Park House
25. Barrowville Townhouse
26. Preston House

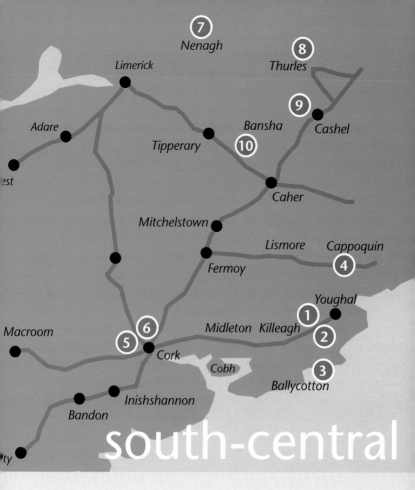

south-central

1. Ballymakeigh Country House
2. Inchiquin House
3. Bayview Hotel
4. Richmond House
5. Hayfield Manor
6. Hotel Isaacs
7. Ashley Park House
8. Inch House
9. Bailey's of Cashel
10. Bansha Castle

# south-west

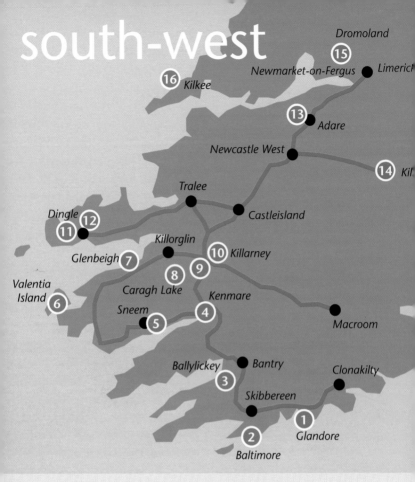

1. Kilfinnan Farm
2. Baltimore Harbour Hotel
3. Sea View House Hotel
4. Muxnaw Lodge
5. Parknasilla
6. Glanleam
7. Ocean View
8. Carrig House
9. Aghadoe Heights Hotel
10. Killarney Great Southern Hotel
11. Greenmount Country House
12. Heatons Country House
13. Dunraven Arms
14. Flemingstown Country House
15. Cahergal Farm & Riding Centre
16. Halpin's Townhouse Hotel

# mid-west

1. Ashley Park House
2. Cahergal Farmhouse & Riding Centre
3. Halpin's Townhouse Hotel
4. Galway Radisson SAS Hotel
5. Iverna Cottage
6. Ross Lake House Hotel
7. Joyce's Waterloo House
8. Delphi Mountain Resort & Spa
9. Ardmore House Hotel
10. Rosturk Woods
11. Pontoon Bridge Hotel
12. Clonalis
13. Viewmount House

# county carlow

Carlow is a low-rise busy midlands Town, on the River Barrow, and was an Anglo Norman stronghold at the edge of a very Gaelic county. Its present calm and serene atmosphere belies its turbulent past. At its heart is a beautiful classical Courthouse with the portico modelled on the Parthenon. Also worth seeing in Carlow is the controversial Regency Gothic Cathedral designed by Pugin. For those interested in Irish brew the Celtic Brewing Company, beside the Railway Station, is worth a tour. The beers brewed there are based on traditional Celtic recipes including a wheat beer, red ale and stout. Carlow has become a commuter town from Dublin and is developing rapidly, hence a plethora of new boutiques, restaurants, bars and cafes. Lennons and La Strada on Tullow Street are good buzzy spots with decent food. Teach Dolmen, also in Tullow Street, has impromptu traditional Irish music sessions. Two miles east of town on the R726 is Browneshill Dolmen, possibly the largest Neolithic stone

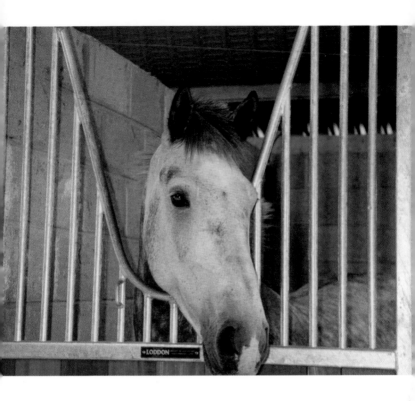

formation in Europe dating from 2500 BC. Seven miles south of
Carlow on the N 9 is Leighlinbridge, the birthplace of Cardinal
Cullen. Altamont Gardens near Tullow and Ballon are beautiful
and attract many visitors. Borris, St. Mullins and the South Leinster
Way are very popular with walkers and cyclists and are a great
weekend destination. Carlow is mainly a farming county, which
accounts for its easy going and generous atmosphere.

"You'll never plough a field by turning it over in your mind"
(Irish Proverb)

# barrowville town house

Randal and Marie Dempsey's beautiful Barrowville Townhouse is a gracious and charming oasis in an otherwise mediocre world of B. & B's in Carlow Town. The house is magnificently furnished and, when you arrive on their doorstep on the Kilkenny Road, you will know with full and certain delight that you have made the right choice. Randal has an artistic eye and cannot resist a fine painting or good sculpture, whilst Marie is delightfully warm and friendly, bustling around ensuring you have every comfort. We were only too delighted to sit at the garden table with a cool drink before setting off to review a Restaurant – it certainly put us in good humour anyway. I have stayed in different rooms in the house, all wonderfully comfortable, but one in particular is quite splendid running from front to back. Breakfast is served each morning in the prettiest raised conservatory off the Drawingroom, and is a spectacular feast in itself. Everything that you could possibly think of is

available from fresh raspberries, loganberries, mueslies, juices, dried fruits, fresh fruits, smoked salmon plates, cheeses, cold meats, and then we get down to the hot food. I would drive this minute to Carlow for Marie Dempsey's poached eggs on potato cakes, complete with chives and slivers of mushroom.

I tried to emulate them but failed miserably. This is a super place too for exploring Kilkenny and you can then return to the peace of Barrowville. There are lots of new Restaurants now in Carlow within walking distance of Barrowville. Children over 12 welcome.

| | |
|---|---|
| Owners | Randal and Marie Dempsey |
| Address | Kilkenny Road, Carlow Co Carlow. |
| Tel / Fax | 059 9143324 /059 9141953 |
| No. Of rooms | 7 |
| Price Double: | €80 |
| Single: | €50 |
| Dinner | No |
| Open | All Year |
| Credit Cards | Visa MC Amex |
| Directions | On right hand side heading south out of Carlow town on N9 |
| Email | barrowvilletownhouse@eircom.net |
| | www.lucindaosullivan.com/barrowvillehouse |

□ P ✗' ▨

# sherwood park house

**M**y happiest days as child were spent at my Aunt's farm, The Grange, in Tullow, Co. Carlow. Hours were spent running up and down the avenue under the big dark overhanging trees. The best swing in the world was a branch of a big horse chestnut tree on the lawn and days were spent "driving" a rusty old tractor skeleton. My cousins would come from England and for them too memories of The Grange remain precious. Tullow is a pretty town with a statue in the square erected to Fr. John Murphy who was "brutally put to death by the British". Uncle Tom took a visiting brother in law from England into the town for a pint, and when the poor man saw the inscription on the statue he thought he would never get back to the safety of Birmingham. He never returned to Ireland.

### SHERWOOD PARK HOUSE
Fancy a candlelit dinner, brass and canopy beds, half testers and fourposters, in a unique early Georgian residence on its own Estate just over an hour from Dublin – you do – well Sherwood Park House at Ballon is the perfect answer. Maureen and Patrick

Owens' lovely house is full of hospitality and friendliness. Maureen is used to entertaining and only wants people to enjoy themselves. Patrick has a great sense of humour. Built in 1700 by Arthur Bailie, Sherwood Park nestles in rolling parklands. The yellow hall, a colour used only by bright optimistic people, sports a piano under the elegant winding staircase and after maybe, when you have had the odd glass or ten, you might feel like tinkling the ivories before pretending to be Moll Flanders upstairs. Dinner is served at a communal table in the lovely old diningroom. Maureen's dinners are based on fresh local farm produce the very best lamb and beef. Sherwood is assigned to Feile Bia so you are assured of quality and you are welcome to bring your own wine and favourite tipples. Smoking, thanks be to God, is not allowed in the diningroom or bedrooms. Pets are allowed outside. The famous Altamont Gardens are nearby and there is excellent fishing on the Slaney. Shooting parties can be arranged locally.

| | |
|---|---|
| Owners | Patrick and Maureen Owens |
| Address | Ballon ,Co Carlow |
| Tel / Fax | 059 9159117 /059 9159355 |
| No. Of rooms | 5 |
| Price, Double: | €90 |
| Single: | €55 |
| Dinner | Yes - BYO wine |
| Open | All Year |
| Credit Cards | Visa Amex MC |
| Directions | Take R705 from Bagenalstown to Borris 4 miles on house on left |
| Email | info@sherwoodparkhouse.ie |
| | www.lucindaosullivan.com/sherwoodparkhouse |

*the step house*

We tied the knot in St. Mullins, a tiny village in South Carlow, where my Uncle was the Parish Priest. The area is known as the Killarney of the east because of its pretty villages, Graiguenamanagh, Borris, Inistiogue, and it is quite easy to get lost between them. I was already staying in St. Mullins before the wedding, but Brendan and his party were coming down on the day in three cars. Their first mishap was at Naas when they stopped to buy film. Each thought the groom was in the other car and he ended up running down the main street as the cars disappeared out of sight. The Gardai came to the rescue and they set off siren wailing … As if he hadn't already learnt his lesson, they stopped again at Borris, this time to change into the "wedding suit" and then found they were totally lost. Frantic calls arrived at the Parochial House – the wedding was two hours late…

James and Cait Coady's creeper clad, yellow fronted, Georgian house in the centre of Borris was originally part of the Borris Estate, ancestral home to the Kings of Leinster. Furnished lavishly throughout with antiques, the house is extremely comfortable, stylish and atmospheric. The drawing room is beautiful and bedrooms are elegant with the Master Bedroom sporting a beautiful four-poster bed. The Coady's own the bar next door so you won't have far to go for a pint of the Black Stuff and you won't have to drive anywhere afterwards either. Actually they also own the very well known Tynan's Bridge Bar in Kilkenny City.

22

Breakfast in summer, weather permitting, is served on the decking in the garden beside the diningroom, and it is just blissful sitting there in the peace and quiet of a summer's morn. The Step House is ideally located in the centre of the Carlow/ Kilkenny/New Ross triangle and is an ideal base, or just lovely for a weekend away. As we go to press plans are ahead to add extra bedrooms all with views of Mount Leinster and the Blackstairs Mountains. Borris has a 9 hole Golf Course, the new Gowran Park Golf Club is ten minutes away, not to mention the Jack Nicklaus designed course at Mount Juliet and the Christy O'Connor, Jnr designed course at Mount Wolesley at Tullow. If you're fancy is for fishing, walking, golfing, or eating and drinking, this is now a very popular area with plenty of variety and fun on offer.

| Owners | James and Cait Coady |
|---|---|
| Address | 66 Main Street, Borris, Co Carlow |
| Tel / Fax | 059 97732 09 /059 9773395 |
| No. Of rooms | 5 |
| Price, Double: | €90 |
| Single: | |
| Dinner | No |
| Open | March 17th – December 23rd |
| Credit Cards | Visa |
| Directions | In Borris Village |
| Email | cait@thestephouse.com |
| | www.lucindaosullivan.com/thestephouse |

# county clare

County Clare is bordered by Galway to the north – the Atlantic to the west and the River Shannon on the east and south. Renowned as a stronghold of traditional music, it also offers many other attractions to the visitor. The Burren is a stark expanse of moonlike grey limestone and shale which is home to the most extraordinary flora and fauna and is a must visit. Kilkee is a seaside resort popular with families and scuba divers and has plenty of restaurants and pubs. Lahinch with its fabulous broad beach attracts surfers and boasts a magnificent golf course. The Cliffs of Moher attract a number of visitors as does the town of Doolin, four miles from the Cliffs. Doolin is for many the music centre of the west and you are sure to find some kind of merriment in one of the town's pubs (O'Connor's, McCann's and McDermott's). If you are unmarried and visit Lisdoonvarna in the month of September you may well find yourself "Spoken For" before you leave, for the town is famous for its month long Matchmaking Festival which comes after the Harvest has been saved.

> Wedlock – "the deep, deep peace of the double bed after the hurly burly of the chaise longue"
>
> (Mrs. Patrick Campbell)

# cahergal farmhouse & riding centre

N oreen McInerney was a Nurse but, when you visit, hopefully you will not be receiving medical attention from her but what I can guarantee is that you will be on the receiving end of the most genuine hospitality. Cahergal Farmhouse is the most recently built house recommended in my Lttle Black Book. The ink on my pages and the paint on the walls of Cahergal I suspect will probably dry at the same time. However, Noreen and Michael Mc Inerney are no newcomers to the hospitality game for they ran a delightful and very successful B&B and a traditional style self-catering house where, incidentally, Michael's 9 aunts, who all became nuns, were born and reared. This must surely be a record. During the past year this dynamic couple have completely converted their home to a first class Guesthouse and Riding Centre on the banks of the River Fergus, close to Dromoland Castle. In Irish terms, they have put their money where their mouths are and they are a breath of fresh air with vision and courage. Five spacious bedrooms have king sized

beds, large T.V. screens and excellent bathrooms. Naturally on a farm in The Golden Vale one would expect the cream of the land in terms of good country food, and that is precisely what you will get at Cahergal Farmhouse. Home made soups and breads followed by the best of meat and fish, delicious rhubarb tarts made with produce straight out of the garden. Come to think of it Noreen whipped up a tart while I lazily sat in the kitchen chatting to Michael (former master of the Clare Hunt) about the next day's riding. If I were the Chief Executive of Failte Ireland, I would rest happy in my bed knowing that Cahergal was the first port of call for many visitors arriving into Shannon airport

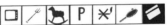

| | |
|---|---|
| Owners | Michael and Noreen McInerney |
| Address | Newmarket-on-Fergus, Co. Clare. |
| Tel / Fax | 061 368358/061 368805 |
| No. Of rooms | 5 |
| Price, Double: | €90-€100 |
| Single: | |
| Dinner | Yes |
| Open | 1st January – 1st December |
| Credit Cards | Visa. M.C. |
| Directions | |
| Email | cahergal@eircom.net |

www.lucindaosullivan.com/cahergalfarm

# halpins townhouse hotel

Halpin's Townhouse Hotel is located in the centre of Kilkee and is owned and run by Pat Halpin who enjoys a great reputation for providing excellent service and comfort in all his enterprises. With Mr. Halpin's exacting standards, the Hotel has been completely revamped and now offers all modern facilities and comforts in compact, perfectly fitted out bedrooms, which incorporate T.V.s hairdryers, hospitality trays with mineral water, tea and coffee making facilities. Kilkee is a busy Victorian holiday town set in a horseshoe bay and is ideal as a base for touring Clare, visiting the Burren and the Cliffs of Moher. There is a magnificent beach set below a dramatic cliff which meets the Duggerna Rocks and, when the tide is out, deep clear pollock holes form and are filled with marine life. The cliff walks around the Town are fantastic and Kilkee is a great place too for scuba diving, snorkeling or visiting the Waterworld. Golfers can play the local 18 hole Kilkee Golf course on one day and head off for the Greg Norman designed Doonbeg Golf Club, Lahinch, Ballybunion or the multifarious other courses during a week's holiday. There is an atmospheric bar in the basement with a glowing fire and plenty of craic and here the day's play can be discussed over a pint - who fades, draws or, God Help us, sockets. You will be amply wined and dined in the Hotel's Vittle's Restaurant. Children over 5 are welcome at Halpin's Townhouse and babysitting can be arranged if you want to escape the little darlings for a while. For the Golfer, the Snorkler or the Kid – or are they all the same – Halpin's Townhouse is lovely for a break.

| Owners | Pat Halpin |
|---|---|
| Address | Erin Street ,Kilkee ,Co Clare |
| Tel / Fax | 065 9056032 /065 9056317 |
| No. Of rooms | 15 |
| Price, Double: | €89-€129 |
| Single: | €69-€89 |
| Dinner | Yes - Restaurant |
| Open | March 15th –31st October |
| Credit Cards | Visa MC Amex Diners |
| Directions | In centre of Kilkee town |
| Email | halpinshotel@iol.ie |
| | www.lucindaosullivan.com/halpinshotel |

# county cork

Known as the Rebel County, for past deeds and the fact that Michael Collins was a native, Cork is the largest county in Ireland. An area of lush fertile farming land, and of fabulously indented coastline, it is also site of Ireland's second City. On the eastern side of the county there is the impressive little fishing port of Ballycotton. Close by is Shanagarry Pottery which is well worth a visit. Further along the coast is the historic town of Cobh, the harbour from which thousands of Irish emigrants departed for the U.S. and Australia, and was the last port of call of the ill fated Titanic. Close by Cobh is Fota Wildlife Park and, not far away, is a spot close to the heart of most Irish men – Midleton – the home of Jameson's Irish whiskey. Travel further west and visit Blarney Castle where you can kiss the famed Blarney Stone, said to endow one with the gift of the gab. Kinsale with its impressive Forts, narrow streets, and yachting marina is a picturesque town, which advertises itself as being the gourmet capital of Ireland. Moving on west through Clonakilty you come to Rosscarbery, with its lovely Continental type village square, but swing left off the main road and wend your way to magnificent Glandore. Stop, take a seat by the wall, overlooking the water and have lunch. Take it easy and enjoy the peace. Further West is the nautically inclined very popular Baltimore. Travel on to Bantry Town which overlooks the famous bay of the same name and you can visit magnificent Bantry House, home of many art treasures. Move on then to the lushness and splendour of Ballylicky and Glengarriff, the last stop before entering the Kingdom of Kerry. And what about Cork City you might ask, for we Dubliners know that Cork is the "real" capital of Ireland. It is a major port on the estuary of the River Lee and this both lively and relaxed City is one of the most pleasurable urban areas in Ireland and is the south's self proclaimed cultural capital. This beautiful county with its rich pastoral land and its rugged coastline of beautiful bays and inlets has many places of historic and cultural interest and the natives are very friendly.

"Culture is roughly anything we do and monkeys don't"
(Lord Raglan)

# ballymakeigh country house

As if on cue, 200 glorious Friesian cows trundled from the fields, in what seemed like a never-ending line for milking, as we arrived at Ballymakeigh House. Margaret and Michael Browne's lovely 300-year-old Farmhouse has won every award in the book and continues to do so. Not just has the house won awards but Margaret, who is Cork's answer to Superwoman, has been Housewife of the Year, T.V. Chef and published her own best selling cookery book "Through My Kitchen Window". Ballymakeigh is a fun place because Margaret and Mike are absolutely irrepressible and love nothing more than a bit of hilarity and craic, meantime cosseting and providing the best of food. This is a very interesting old house furnished with antiques. The bedrooms, however, have every modern facility and comfort, stylishly furnished and draped with, as Margaret might say herself, "bags of old fashioned comfort" and have, of course, perfectly fitted and kitted out bathrooms. If you are feeling energetic, there is a hard tennis court, or you can walk the land, see the milking parlour, or merely sit down in the lovely big conservatory for the day with a glass in hand. Americans love to visit "real Irish" homes and this I can tell you is a "real Irish" home but with everything running to perfection right down to the ice machine. A spanking

dinner is served in the lovely old world red
diningroom Breakfasts are hearty with fresh
pressed apple juice, fruits and yogurts,
traditional grainy porridge with spices, cereals,
kippers with thyme, and a super "Full Irish"
including rashers, sausages, Clonakilty pudding,
tomatoes and eggs. Preserves, of course, are
homemade as are the breads - traditional soda bread and leek and
onion savoury scones are to die for. Mark my words, like me, you
will go back again and again to Ballymakeigh.

| | |
|---|---|
| Owners | Margaret Browne |
| Address | Ballymakeigh House, Killeagh,Co. Cork, Ireland |
| Tel / Fax | 024 95184 /024 95370 |
| No. Of rooms | 6 |
| Price, Double: | €90-€100 |
| Single: | €55 |
| Dinner | €39 |
| Open | All year |
| Credit Cards | Visa MC Amex |
| Directions | Located 1 mile off N25. 22 miles east of Cork City Sign posted in Killeagh village at Old Thatch Pub |
| Email | ballymakeigh@eircom.net |
| | www.lucindaosullivan.com/ballymakeighhouse |

# baltimore harbour hotel

altimore is a fishing village at the very south of Ireland, spectacularly located looking out to Roaringwater Bay and the Carbery Islands. It is about as far south and out into the water as you can get. A magnet for the "yachties", particularly in July and August during regatta time, so accommodation is at a premium. In Baltimore there is a Sailing club, two Sailing Schools and two Diving Schools and water is the key word here. Whilst the "junior yachties" are learning the ropes, Mum and Dad can relax and enjoy the local amenities and facilities at The Baltimore Harbour Hotel. Ideally located overlooking the harbour, the Hotel has had a major revamp for 2004. It has 64 lovely bedrooms, a 16m swimming pool, bubble pool, children's pool, and sauna, steam room, treatment rooms for massage and reflexology. We really loved the two and three bed roomed courtyard suites at the hotel. These suites are not self catering but do have a spacious lounge/kitchen area with a kettle, fridge and microwave and some have balconies. We stayed with our two teenage sons and found the "suite" idea wonderful because when we wanted to socialize in the hotel they could stay behind and watch "Friends" without just being confined to a bedroom. Food at the hotel's Clipper Restaurant is excellent using the best of local West Cork fresh produce and plenty of seafood – think Crab Claw Salad with Citrus dressing or Fresh Tuna Steak on a bed of squid ink Tagliatelle with tomato Herb Sauce. The staff are very obliging and will cater for all needs. They have a comprehensive children's menu. There are a number of interesting pubs and cafes in Baltimore and ferries leave each day to Cape Clear, which has incredible bird life, and for Sherkin Island with its two lovely sandy

beaches. The hotel's Chartroom Bar has music sessions in summer and at weekends or, alternatively, you might enjoy sitting in the local square with a cool drink watching the sun go down over the islands. Paradise Regained.

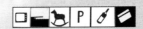

| | |
|---|---|
| Owners | Charles Cullinane |
| Address | Baltimore ,Co Cork, Ireland |
| Tel / Fax | 028 20361 /028 20466 |
| No. Of rooms | 64 |
| Price, Double: | €120-€168 |
| Single: | |
| Dinner | Restaurant |
| Open | February – 21st December |
| Credit Cards | All major Cards |
| Directions | Sign posted on the right on entry to Baltimore from Skibbereen |
| Email | info@baltimoreharbourhotel.ie www.lucindaosullivan.com/baltimoreharbourhotel |

# bayview hotel

allycotton is a completely unspoiled Fishing Village in East Cork dating back to 1250 AD. Not only is it completely unspoiled but it is also largely undiscovered save by those in the know, for people tend to dash on further west to the more overblown high profile villages. Once you turn down at Castlemartyr you whirl around the back roads amongst high hedges and fertile fields which are eons away from the modern world – and yet so near. Ballycotton is an ideal base for visiting Cork, if you prefer to stay out of a City, or for taking a leisurely tour of Stephen Pearce's Pottery and for visiting Ballymaloe, Cobh and the Jameson Irish Whiskey Centre at Midleton, after which you might need to be careful on the Ballycotton Cliff Walk!!

## BAYVIEW HOTEL BALLYCOTTON

I have had a problem for a number of years with Hotels and Restaurants, a problem which can spoil one's entire visit – namely – the "back room" and the "table beside the toilet door respectively. I have been offered a far from romantic attic in Paris, a box in London beside a lift shaft with pneumatic drills working in it, no sea view all over the place, a room over the rubbish exit in Palma and even rooms with no view at all save the sidewall of the next building. The Bayview Hotel in my eyes is just perfectly designed, for all the rooms have magnificent sea views. As you look out it feels more like a "visual tour" because you are just over the sheer drop onto the rocks, gazing out into infinity, broken

only by the old world little quaint Ballycotton Harbour. Not only does the Bayview have 35 perfect rooms, a comfortable library style bar and lounge, it has excellent food provided by Head Chef, Ciaran Scully, who cooks up the best of French style food in The Capricho Restaurant in this special little Hotel. There are six golf courses within 30 minutes drive, as well as some of the best sea angling in Europe. Stephen Belton provides a 5 star service at the 4 star Bayview. Go and discover it for yourself.

| | |
|---|---|
| Owners | Stephen Belton, General Manager. |
| Address | Ballycotton, Co Cork, Ireland. |
| Tel / Fax | 021 4646746 /021 4646075 |
| No. Of rooms | 35 |
| Price, Double: | € 160 -€194 |
| Single: | €112-€129 |
| Dinner | Restaurant |
| Open | March - October |
| Credit Cards | All major Cards |
| Directions | Located in Ballycotton Village |
| Email | info@bayviewhotel.net |
| | www.lucindaosullivan.com/bayviewhotel |

hayfield manor

"Thelma and Louise" said Margaret Naughton, General Manager, of the 5 Star Hayfield Manor Hotel as she both welcomed and helped the windblown disheveled pair scramble out of the low open topped car with their bags. It is not very often that the General Manager of any Hotel is at the door to greet one – they are usually hiding away in their Offices leaving the front of house stuff to their minions. I must say it was very impressive and this hands on approach clearly results in a very high standard of performance all round. Hayfield Manor, a member of the Small Luxury Hotels of the World, is where the Legal fraternity rest their briefs when in Cork – and believe me they like their comforts. Hayfield is a red bricked neo-Georgian building set on two acres of ground with mature trees surrounded by a 15-foot wall. Located beside the University it has a beautiful Spa, Pool and Beauty Salon. The first impression is "oh, its so pretty" – like a Connecticut Mansion in an American movie – everything perfect with a lovely old picturesque tree right outside the front door, topiary planters, carriage lights, and a liveried doorman. The bedrooms are beautifully draped and lavishly furnished – you

would really want to hibernate in them but what we wanted, after driving all day, was a drink and this came with oysters and canapés. There is an air of being cushioned away from the real world at Hayfield and, although it is 5 star, it is absolutely unpretentious. Fabulous food is served in The Manor Room Restaurant by Executive Chef, Philippe Farineau - Marble Terrine of Foie Gras layered with poached figs, dried pears; Filet Mignon of Dutch Veal, Truffle Risotto, roasted asparagus with artichoke with truffle sauce. The Bar also serves what I would call Bistro food with all the trimmings, as opposed to what most people think of as Bar Food, and is an occasion in itself. Greek Salad, Confit of Duck with onion marmalade and Monte Carlo Potatoes or Freshly Caught Seafood and appropriate wines. Hayfield, a wonderful luxurious oasis in Cork only a mile from Patrick Street is the perfect place for business or pleasure. Enquire too about their special breaks. I just want to live permanently in the picture postcard world of Hayfield Manor.

| | |
|---|---|
| Owners | Margaret Naughton, General Manager. |
| Address | Perrott Avenue, College Road, Cork |
| Tel / Fax | 021 4845900 /021 4316839 |
| No. Of rooms | 88 |
| Price, Double: Single: | €300 |
| Dinner | Yes Restaurant and Bar Menu |
| Open | All Year |
| Credit Cards | Visa, MC, Amex ,Diners |
| Directions | Signed off College Road |
| Email | enquiries@hayfieldmanor.ie |

www.lucindaosullivan.com/hayfieldmanor

# hotel isaacs

The idea for Hotel Isaacs was inspired. A vast, red-bricked, Victorian landmark building on Cork's MacCurtain Street, used by Nat Ross Removals, was converted into Hotel Isaacs offering great value accommodation in excellent surroundings. An oasis of calm, entered through a cobblestone archway, the lobby has beautiful original paintings as have the bedrooms. Hotel Isaacs always had a reputation for meticulous housekeeping but has now undergone a major refurbishment and the bedrooms, which are very modern bright, airy and comfortable, have had a total revamp. Fourteen new non smoking Superior Rooms have been added which, apart from all the standard comforts, are ideally suited for the technophile – modems, safes, minibars, eu/usa built in adaptors, ISDN phone line, air-conditioning, trouser press, iron and ironing board. The location is great, for Hotel Isaac's is surrounded by Restaurants, clubs, pubs, boutiques, and antique and décor shops, now in the area. The Hotel has its own excellent buzzy Restaurant, Greene's under the baton of French Chef, Frederic Deformeau, which overlooks a floodlit cascading feature waterfall, so you are ideally placed for a fun gourmet weekend – park the car and forget about it. Weather permitting food and drinks can be enjoyed in the courtyard. Hotel Isaacs is very close to Cork Railway Station. There are also 11 two and three bedroom apartments adjacent to the Hotel, which are popular with small groups, families and business people who like a bit more space and freedom.

| | |
|---|---|
| Owners | Paula Lynch, General Manager. |
| Address | 48 MacCurtain Street, Cork. |
| Tel / Fax | 021 4500011/021 4506355 |
| No. Of rooms | 47 |
| Price, Double/Twin | €100 - €160 |
| Double Superior | €140 - €210 |
| Single | €72 - €150 |
| Triple | €138- €228 |
| Dinner | Restaurant |
| Open | All year – except 24/25/26 December |
| Credit Cards | Visa. M.C. Amex |
| Directions | From Patrick Street follow Directions to Cork Railway Station. Hotel on left in one-way traffic system. |
| Email | cork@isaacs.ie |
| | www.lucindaosullivan.com/hotelisaacs |

# kilfinnan farm

Along the south west coastline of West Cork, which is a myriad of little bays and creeks, sandy coves, tidal loughs and magical ocean sprays, is Glandore, a glorious coastal village comprising a little harbour, a couple of pubs, a small hotel, and a Restaurant high on the hill. So enticing is Glandore that it surely got separated from its Italian mother during the ice age, landing instead on Irish shores to bring a little continental glamour. It is spectacularly beautiful and a magnet for wealthy Dublin and Cork people. Glandore is relatively undiscovered by Tourists who "don't turn down" but keep going on the main road through Leap (pronounced Lep) like the clappers heading further West not realizing that the whole point of West Cork and Kerry is to amble and socialise, not race through it. They don't know what they are missing. The two pubs that pretty well make up Glandore have tables by a low wall on this natural "terrace" but if you don't get there early in the summertime you have had it. The whole point about Glandore is not just to admire the view but to "people watch". You sit there, with your friends, enjoying pretty sandwiches from "Hayes Bar" for as long as possible, observing the top of the range cars and their drivers cruise slowly through …

# KILFINNAN FARMHOUSE

Accommodation in Glandore is at a premium but just an Irish mile away, high up overlooking Glandore Harbour, is Margaret Mehigan's lovely family run Kilfinnan Farmhouse which, apart from being lovely, offers super, very reasonably priced, accommodation. The sweet old ivy clad house has four en suite bedrooms with really comfortable beds, crisp bedlinen and pretty views, some overlooking the old world garden. You are likely to

meet the cows being brought in for milking as you arrive whilst Margaret, meantime, envelopes you in the warmth of her welcome. Don't expect foil covered butters and shop bought marmalade at Kilfinnan for everything is beautifully presented in pretty dishes and milk, eggs, meat, fruit and vegetables are freshly produced on the farm so you can only benefit. Kilfinnan is surrounded by pretty little beaches which for the most part of the year are virtually unoccupied. There are all sorts of water based activities nearby – water-skiing, sailing, and diving down to look at all the wrecks which came a cropper. The stunningly impressive Bronze Age Drombeg stone circle, made up of a formation of seventeen stones, is just across the fields leading down to the water. Nearby there is also a fulacht fiadh, which is an ancient cooking site where troughs of water would have been heated by hot stones thrown into them from a fire. Kilfinnan Farm is a real find in a real Ireland – don't tell anyone.

| | |
|---|---|
| Owners | Margaret Mehigan |
| Address | Glandore, Co Cork. |
| Tel / Fax | 028 33233 |
| No. Of rooms | 4 |
| Price, Double: | €70 |
| Single: | €45 |
| Dinner | No |
| Open | All Year |
| Credit Cards | No |
| Directions | Take R597 towards Glandore Watch for sign to left for house |
| Email | kilfinnanfarm@eircom.net |
| | www.lucindaosullivan.com/kilfinnanfarm |

# sea view house hotel

"Yes, we do breakfast in bed … if necessary," said the wonderful Kathleen O'Sullivan, Proprietress of the Sea View House Hotel at Ballylickey, in response to my timorous enquiry on the telephone the night before. We felt like two naughty schoolgirls – but yes, they did breakfast in bed all right and, as one would expect under Kathleen O'Sullivan's eagle eye, it arrived on the button of 8 a.m. and was just perfect. A new wing has recently been added to the Sea View House, along with a magnificent French classical style round "conservatory" to the dining room, and it is just a fab place to stay. All of the rooms are splendid with larger rooms being absolutely divine – some

opening out to the gardens – beautifully furnished with antiques, French Armoires and headboards, wonderful paintings – each different and each special. We had arrived like two exhausted rats into the hall of the Sea View having driven in and out of every peninsula from Cork to

Ballylickey. Make no mistake this takes hours, but I don't feel I have had my fix of West Cork each Summer without doing it. Having showered and dickied ourselves up we went down the corridor past Kathleen O'Sullivan's "Command Centre". "You look very nice", she said to my companion – "go through that door there and you can have a drink". Having passed muster we went into a cocktail bar and armed ourselves with suitable Sherries and set down to peruse the menus. The food is excellent – think Sauté Lamb kidneys Madeira sauce, whisper light Scampi or avocado with real Dublin Bay Prawns, Rack of Lamb or lemon sole all perfectly produced and served. "Do we get both Puddings and Cheese?" asked a young Englishman sitting across from us with his wife. His eyes lighting up like a child's when given the affirmative answer. We all looked together at a Victor Meldrew look-alike who passed by us and the young man said "we feel very young" – "so do we", we chimed sharply" to this mere fresh faced youth. Sea View House Hotel is brilliant.

| Owners | Kathleen O Sullivan |
|---|---|
| Address | Ballylickey, Bantry, Co Cork |
| Tel / Fax | 027 50073 /027 51555 |
| No. Of rooms | 25 |
| Price, Double: | €140 -€175 |
| Single: | None |
| Family: | €175 |
| Dinner | Yes |
| Open | Mid March-Mid November |
| Credit Cards | All major cards |
| Directions | Located on main road from Bantry to Glengarriff |
| Email | info@seaviewhousehotel.com |

www.lucindaosullivan.com/seaviewhousehotel

# inchiquin house

At some stage in our lives we all have a vision of discovering a gorgeous house tucked away in the countryside, as well furnished and as comfortable as our own home, and being able to play house there for a week or two without any of the responsibilities. It is not easy but I have found such a precious gem, Inchiquin House. Michael and Margaret Browne are perfectionists so the house is lovingly restored. Big and spacious this Victorian 5 bed roomed house has beds that are only equaled in comfort with the beds in their other establishment the nearby Ballymakeigh House. The house has 4 bathrooms and a very functional kitchen facing west. The kitchen and dining room are the focal points of the house by day, and the large sitting room with open fire is there to while away the night in comfort. Expect a welcome pack of Ballymakeigh Preserves and Bread on arrival. It is conveniently located at the end of a tree-lined avenue off N25 - 20 miles east of Cork City- 2 miles from Youghal.

| | |
|---|---|
| Owners | Margaret Browne |
| Address | Ballymakeigh House, Killeagh, Co Cork |
| Tel / Fax | 024 95184 /024 95370 |
| No. Of rooms | 5 |
| Price, Double: | This is self catering 4 Star house |
| Single: | €500 –€800 per week |
| Dinner | Available at Ballymakeigh House |
| Open | All Year |
| Credit Cards | Visa MC |
| Directions | Ring for directions |
| Email | ballymakeigh@eircom.net |
| | www.lucindaosullivan.com/inchiquin |

# county donegal

From the Inishowen peninsula in the north, to the sweeping beaches of the south, Donegal with its two hundred mile coastline has scenery that is unsurpassed throughout the country and is well worth a tour. Enter Donegal from the south through the popular bucket and spade holiday resort of Bundoran and travel north through Laghey before reaching Donegal Town where you may visit O'Donnell Castle. Continue around to Dunkineely with its fabulous St. John's Point and then on to Killybegs, Ireland's most successful fishing village. Onwards and upwards will bring you to Glencolumbcille and its numerous megalithic remains and nearby folk village and museum. Rejoin the N56 which winds its way northwards through Ardara, Glenties, Dungloe, and the Irish speaking Gweedore and Gortahork. The road turns southwards at Dunfanaghy, leave the N56 and go further east to the sweeping Lough Swilly and southwards through Rathmullan, to the pretty Ramelton on the banks of the salmon rich River Leannan. Continue on to Letterkenny, the county's largest town, and site of St. Eunan's Cathedral and onwards to Lifford the county town close to the Northern Ireland border town of Strabane. I should mention that Donegal has the highest seacliffs in Europe at Slieve League. Don't forget the Rosses, an area which includes Kincaslough from whence Ireland's most popular balladeer comes, and where hundreds of people flock every year to his home for the annual tea party with Daniel O'Donnell and his mother.

*"A folk singer is someone who sings through his nose by ear"*
(anon)

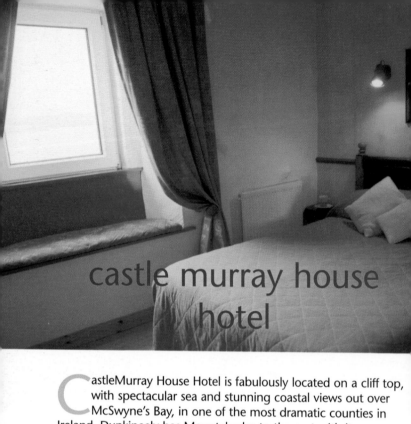

# castle murray house hotel

CastleMurray House Hotel is fabulously located on a cliff top, with spectacular sea and stunning coastal views out over McSwyne's Bay, in one of the most dramatic counties in Ireland. Dunkineely has Mountcharles to the east with its sea angling centre and boats available for hire and, to the west, Killybegs, probably Ireland's busiest fishing village. The ruins of McSwyne's Castle are owned by the Hotel and are floodlit at night which adds to an already wonderful inherently brilliant atmosphere. The word Hotel conjures up Modern 4 Star with Leisure Centre but CastleMurray is far more intimate than that – more inns and havens feel which are not words used very much in Ireland but do describe very well a good Restaurant with excellent accommodation and atmosphere. The ten bedrooms are all en-suite, furnished individually, and have digital T.V. and all facilites. One room is done in African style with black African carved face masks, giraffe cushions with leopard skin lampshades – you can fantasise you are on Safari though I would prefer to be here in Donegal – another room with a pretty window seat is beautifully decorated in colorful coral. CastleMurray is a very comfortable and relaxing spot. Have a jar in the little bar before and after

dinner – you can relax as you are not going to have to drive anywhere. Meals can be served outside on the verandah in the Summer. The food is wonderful – pick your own lobster out of a tank – prawns, scallops, crab and don't forget to finish up with the Prune and Armagnac parfait.....it is to die for.

| Owners | Marguerite Howley |
| Address | St Johns Point, Dunkineely, Co Donegal. |
| Tel / Fax | 074 9737022 /074 9737330 |
| No. Of rooms | 10 |
| Price, Double: | €116- €140 |
| Single: | |
| Dinner | Yes |
| Open | Mid February- Mid January. Closed Monday low season. Open every day high season |
| Credit Cards | Visa MC Diners Amex |
| Directions | 2 Kms from Dunkineely village |
| Email | castlemurray@eircom.net |
| | www.lucindaosullivan.com/castlemurray |

# coxtown manor

S ome of the best Restaurants in Europe are in Belgium but none of our M.E.P.s like to tell us this because they want us to think they are working so hard traveling back and forth to Brussels. Certainly some of them seem to have added on a few kilos since they started the E.U.commute. One man who has come the other way and set up business in the north West, just outside Donegal Town and close to Donegal Bay, is Eduard Dewael with his fabulous late Georgian House, Coxtown Manor. The location is magnificent, the house is magnificent, the food is magnificent and service and attention are magnificent. I have not met anyone yet who has but raved about Coxtown Manor and this is a place we are going to be hearing a lot more of. The décor is very much of today, stripped floorboards, pretty colours and lovely furniture, adding a continental twist to his striking house. They have a wood panelled bar where you can try out some of the famous Belgian Strong Beers, Duval, Westmalle along with all the customary drinks. Dinner in the Restaurant offers a combination of Belgian/ Irish food or, I suppose you might say, the best of Irish produce cooked with a Belgian slant by Head Chef, Michel Aerts. Their fillet steaks are from the finest locally raised Charolais herds, the lamb is raised on Coxtown grounds, and with the Atlantic Ocean on their doorstep, believe me the fish is good. Eduard uses free-range

eggs, organic red label chicken – nothing but the best of produce. You will die for the famous Belgian chocolate desserts which feature largely on their repertoire. If you are a golfer, you have Donegal, Bundoran and Rosses Point Golf Courses from which to choose. Do a Hercule Poirot and come and investigate their Gourmet Weekends … you won't be disappointed. Oh just think, hot chocolate with a splash of Grand Marnier before you toddle up to bed … oh maybe I'll have another one…

| Owners | Eduard Dewael |
| --- | --- |
| Address | Laghey ,Co Donegal |
| Tel / Fax | 074 9734575 /074 9734576 |
| No. Of rooms | 10 |
| Price, Double: Single: | €70-€110 €135 for family room |
| Dinner | Yes - Restaurant |
| Open | All year except 3 weeks November and 3 weeks January |
| Credit Cards | Visa ,MC |
| Directions | Watch for sign on N15 between Ballyshannon and Donegal town |
| Email | coxtownmanor@oddpost.com |

www.lucindaosullivan.com/coxtownmanor

# frewin

Ramelton is an old plantation town with beautiful Georgian buildings sited on the river Lennan that flows into Lough Swilly. In times past the river was navigable by ocean going vessels and Ramelton was an important town for trade hence the town itself was prosperous and homes were furnished with many exotic imported items. The Fish House, on the Quayside, has a town map listing a number of important buildings worth seeing. Eateries are plentiful and superb fresh fish is widely available.

## FREWIN

Whether in winter or summer, Thomas and Regina Coyle's picture postcard pretty former rectory, Frewin, is a magnificent place to stay. Everything about the house, bedrooms, suites and gardens, have been lovingly restored and enhanced by the owners. Thomas hails from the area and has a knowledge of the countryside which would enthral and keep visitors listening to local folklore for many an hour. Many of the bedrooms are decorated in white with white painted furniture, and muslin curtains. One of the bedrooms is just perfect for honeymooners or a romantic stay, a bridal suite complete with lace drapes over the bed, delicately carved mirrors and beautiful ornaments adorn the room. Throughout, the house has retained its original character, with modern showers fitting in unobtrusively. Thomas and Regina have a great interest in antiques and restoration and there is a little antique shop and a small self-catering cottage in the grounds. The gardens are beautiful. Dinner is available with advance notice and you can

bring your own wine. The dining room is special, no electric lighting, but a really splendid atmosphere under a real candle lit chandelier. Then you can relax after dinner in the lovely library. Thomas and Regina are warm and entertaining hosts. Frewin is a place one doesn't want to leave.

Children over 8 welcome

| | |
|---|---|
| Owners | Thomas & Regina Coyle |
| Address | Ramelton, Co. Donegal. |
| Tel / Fax | 074 9151246/074 9151246 |
| No. Of rooms | 4 |
| Price, Double: | €100 - €140 |
| Twin | €140 |
| Single: | €70-€90 |
| | 1 Bed. Self Catering Cottage €450-€525 per week |
| Dinner | Yes – prior arrangement BYO Wine |
| Open | All year save Christmas |
| Credit Cards | Visa. M.C. |
| Directions | R245 from Letterkenny for 9 miles. Turn right on approaching Ramelton. House on right after 300 yards. |
| Email | flaxmill@indigo.ie www.lucindaosullivan.com/frewin |

# county down

he County is remembered in the popular Percy French Song "Where the mountains of Mourne sweep down to the sea". Apart from the Mournes, there are numerous places of interest to visit in Co. Down. North of the County is the Ulster Folk and Transport Museum one of the best in Northern Ireland. The well-known Bangor seaside resort is a popular vacation area for locals and visitors alike. Follow the shores of the beautiful Strangford Lough towards Downpatrick and its association with Ireland's Patron Saint, St. Patrick. Hillsborough Castle, where the Anglo Irish Agreement, was signed in 1985 is now the residence of the British Secretary of State for Northern Ireland, and tours of the castle are available between April and September. Centred round a beautiful cathedral founded in 500AD, Dromore has a Celtic Cross, town stocks, and a Victorian Viaduct. The County offers a range of outdoor activities, walking, pony trekking, fishing, and golfers will undoubtedly be lured by Newcastle's Royal County Down Golf Course.

*"Give me my Golf Clubs, fresh air and a beautiful partner, and you can keep my golf clubs and the fresh air!"*

( Jack Benny)

# clanmurry

John and Sara McCorkell's Clanmurry is a lovely peaceful traditional Georgian house on six acres of stunning gardens filled with abundant lush shrubs and plants. It is a superb house and location in which to base oneself for visiting Northern Ireland, as it is not far from the border, only four miles from Hillsborough Castle, close to Lough Neagh, and, most importantly, very convenient for the hustle and bustle of Belfast City which is only 20 miles, and 30 minutes, down the A1. Just think of the bliss of escaping city noise and returning to such a glorious haven, or stopping there on the way to the Larne Ferry. Two twin bedrooms with garden views are serenely furnished and John and Sara are delightfully humorous hosts who will be very happy to plan out routes for you. Interestingly the McCorkell family owned a passenger shipping line whose ships took thousands of emigrants across the Atlantic to a new life in America and Canada in the 18th and 19th Centuries. Oil paintings in Clanmurry depict the ships owned by the McCorkell Line of Derry, including the beautiful Mohongo, which made over one hundred crossings of the North Atlantic without serious mishap. The Minnehaha was the McCorkell Line's finest clipper and was known at most ports from Quebec to New Orleans as "The Green Yacht from Derry". There are many Restaurants nearby, probably best booked in advance as they are very popular, and John and Sara will be happy to organize a taxi if you don't want to drive. Breakfast at

Clanmurry is brilliant so forget the old Irish Breakfast when you can be spoiled with Coddled egg or Smoked Haddock and poached egg, or the real Clanmurry specialty, Kedgeree (minimum 2 people) – bring someone, drag someone, but have the Kedgeree you won't get it anywhere else – very Out of Africa– or was it India…. Children Over 12 welcome.

| | |
|---|---|
| Owners | John and Sara McCorkell |
| Address | 16 Lower Quilly Road, Dromore, Co. Down BT25 1NL |
| Tel / Fax | +44 (0)2892693760 /+44(0)2892698106 |
| No. Of rooms | 2 |
| Price, Twin: | Stg 60 |
| Single: | Stg 40 |
| Dinner | No |
| Open | January 2nd –December 20th |
| Credit Cards | Visa, MC |
| Directions | Off M1 take A1 south to Dromore for 8 miles 1st right after only road bridge over Dromore bypass.Entrance first on right |
| Email | mccorkell@btinternet.com |
| | www.lucindaosullivan.com/clanmurry |

# county dublin

County Dublin is dominated by Ireland's Capital City, Dublin. The city exudes the style and confidence of any European Capital but its citizens still know how to party and enjoy themselves like there was no tomorrow. Set on the fine sweep of Dublin Bay, the city is divided by the River Liffey, which flows from west to east. South of the river are the fine examples of Dublin's Georgian past with the lovely Fitzwilliam and Merrion Squares, and the beautiful St. Stephen's Green with its rich and colourful flowerbeds, green lawns, dreamy ponds and shaded walkways. North of the river is the Municipal Art Gallery, the Writers Museum, as well as the Phoenix Park, one of the largest enclosed parks in the world and the residence of the Country's President and the U.S. Ambassador – a favourite haunt of Dubliners. The city abounds with places and buildings that remind us of Ireland's historic and troubled past. The General Post Office was the scene of violent fighting in 1916. Dublin Castle was seat of the British Occupation Control, and Kilmainham Jail has many shadows of the past. Round the Bay to the South the road leads through fashionable Monkstown with its crescent of lively restaurants, on to the town of Dun Laoire with its harbour and yacht clubs, to Sandycove and its association with James Joyce. Further South is the magnificent sweep of Killiney Beach and the homes of many rich and famous. North of the city are some lovely and friendly seaside towns and villages – the very fashionable Malahide, the busy fishing town of Howth, the fine sandy beach of Portmarnock with its famous Golf Links and Skerries, a favourite spot for Dubliners and visitors alike. As the song says … Dublin can be Heaven.

"Other people have a nationality, the Irish and the Jews have a psychosis"

(Brendan Behan)

aberdeen lodge

**Y**ou won't find any "Basil Fawlty's" at Pat Halpin's Aberdeen
Lodge, in the heart of Dublin's leafy embassy belt,
Ballsbridge. Pat, the ultimate Hotelier, quietly misses
nothing, is supremely helpful and efficient whilst, seemingly
effortlessly, running four small private Hotels. Nothing is too much
trouble for the staff at Aberdeen who are motivated to provide the
5 star standard of friendliness and helpfulness expected by the
Head Man. Aberdeen Lodge is a large Edwardian Villa on its own
grounds expertly converted to provide accommodation of the
very highest standard. Fine bedrooms, some with fourposters and
whirlpool spa baths, have satellite T.V. mineral water, trouser press,
all the little details. There is an elegant drawingroom with plenty
to read and you can order from their substantial Drawingroom
and Room Service Menu. They also have a wine list. Breakfast is
brilliant – a lavish buffet displayed in pretty Nicholas Mosse
pottery followed by a hot selection. Breakfast is included in the
room rate but, if you want to have a business meeting over
breakfast, you can invite a guest to join you (approx €15).
Ballsbridge is where the Royal Dublin Society have their
magnificent Showgrounds and is the venue of the famous Dublin
Horse Show. Down the road is Lansdowne Road – the
headquarters of Irish rugby. If you are a resident and your address
is "Dublin 4" that says it all about you – money – class - although

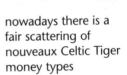

nowadays there is a fair scattering of nouveaux Celtic Tiger money types infiltrating the red bricked roads. Location, location, location is the story at Ballsbridge for you can walk into the centre of Town in 15 minutes, the DART station is nearby at Sydney Parade or taxis will be reasonable as it is so close to Town. The Blue Airport Coach also stops at two Hotels in Ballsbridge so transport is a dream. Cap that all with lots of nearby Restaurants, Thai, Indian, Chinese, French, Mediterranean and you can see what I mean about location. Not suitable for Children under 5. In Dublin for Shopping, Theatre, Rugby Matches, Business or just a break – Aberdeen Lodge is where it is at.

| | | |
|---|---|---|
| Owners | Pat Halpin | |
| Address | 53 Park Avenue ,Ballsbridge,Dublin 4 | |
| Tel / Fax | 01 2838155 / 01 2837877 | |
| No. Of rooms | 19 | |
| Price, Double: | € 130-€160 | |
| Single: | € 90-€125 | |
| Treble: | € 160-€190 | |
| Dinner | Drawing room Menu available all day | |
| Open | All Year | |
| Credit Cards | VS MC Amex Diners | |
| Directions | Down the road from Sydney Parade Dart Station Park Avenue runs parallel with Merrion Road and Strand Road close to RDS | |
| Email | aberdeen@iol.ie | |
| | www.lucindaosullivan.com/aberdeenlodge | |

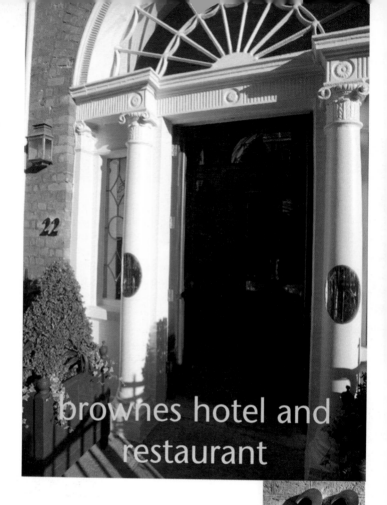

## brownes hotel and restaurant

**B**rowne's Hotel and Restaurant is one of the great recent success stories on the Irish hospitality scene. In a fine Georgian House, the location has to be the most glorious in Dublin, overlooking the beautiful St. Stephen's Green, and close to the famous Shelbourne Hotel, always a hive of Dublin social life, so it is right at the heart of things. Very convenient too for Grafton Street's upmarket shops. Formerly known as Browne's Townhouse and Brasserie founded by Barry Canny, Browne's is now under the umbrella of Spain's very successful Stein Group, which already has a number of Boutique Hotels around Europe, and they are adding their highly successful stamp to an already winning operation. The high ceilinged bedrooms associated with these grand houses are superb, lush plush and beautifully

furnished with stylish bathrooms and accoutrements. On the first floor overlooking the Green is a wonderful junior suite containing Marilyn Monroe's "Murphy Bed", from her New York office, which folds into the wall – quite a gimmick - so this room can be used for receptions, and meetings or just for pushing out the boat when in Dublin. Plush sofas in the small anteroom drawingroom are very inviting for drinks before or after dinner in the large buzzy Restaurant to which Dubliners flock each evening. The Restaurant is on two levels, a long room mirrored on both sides with comfortable banquette seating, an Italian frieze, and a large French chandelier. On the menu you can look forward perhaps to Roast Breast of Guinea Fowl stuffed with foie gras or maybe Ossu Bucco of Veal Shin – the range is always superb. Wonderful staff will make sure your visit to Dublin is memorable.

| | |
|---|---|
| Owners | The Stein Group |
| Address | 22 St. Stephen's Green, Dublin. 2. |
| Tel / Fax | 01 6383939/016383900 |
| No. Of rooms | 11 |
| Price, Double: | €210 -€240 |
| Single: | €170-€185 |
| Family | €250 |
| Suite | €350 |
| Breakfast | €17.50 |
| Dinner | Restaurant |
| Open | All year save Close 24th Dec - 2nd Jan. |
| Credit Cards | Visa MC Diners Amex |
| Directions | On St. Stephen's Green in section between Dawson Street and Kildare Street. |
| Email | info@brownesdublin.com |
| | www.lucindaosullivan.com/browneshotel |

# cedar lodge

In my next life I want to be a poodle living in Cedar Lodge. Well, I don't mind what or whom I will come back as, as long as I can continue to have occasional pampering in this great establishment. Gerard and Mary Doody have the happy knack of making everything about your stay really special. I was first directed their way by a Director in nearby RTE and I will always be in his debt as a result. Guest Books can tell a lot – in one I opened to read and it said "a reportable experience and it will be" and in another country house I read "I must tell my brother Tony (Blair) of this experience". Both places were dreadful. Cedar Lodge's Guest Book too tells a story – page after page of raves- from "Estupendo" to in current day high praise idiom "Wicked" through 100% to "Absolutely Fabulous". I rest my case. I just love the warm welcome, the impeccably kept house, the hint of polish, the beautifully furnished rooms, the cosy and comfortable beds with great

lighting , fluffy towels, and much much more. I would give the Doody's many Stars (I do not give accolades so the Stars would be very special ) but the AA and RAC have beaten me to the post with 5 Stars.

Breakfast is a feast presided over by Gerard with a never ending supply of tea and freshly ground coffee, juices, fruits, rhubarb in season, Irish brown soda bread, pancakes with maple syrup, poached eggs, omelette and so on. Located opposite the British Embassy, close to the Royal Dublin Society Showgrounds, Ballsbridge is really in the hub of things. There are great

Restaurants close by including the Four Seasons Hotel a few yards away. Location Location Location – Cedar Lodge has it.

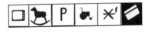

| Owners | Gerard and Mary Doody |
| Address | 98 Merrion Road, Ballsbridge ,Dublin4. |

| Tel / Fax | 01 6684410 /01 6684533 |
| No. Of rooms | 16 |
| Price, Double: | €120 |
| Single: | €90 |
| Dinner | No |
| Open | January 2nd – December 23rd |
| Credit Cards | Visa ,MC ,Amex |
| Directions | Opposite British Embassy on Merrion Road |
| Email | info@cedarlodge.ie |
| | www.lucindaosullivan.com/cedarlodge |

merrion hall

Merrion Hall is the type of Bed and Breakfast establishment that one always longs to find in a big City but usually fails to. It is a fine substantial impeccably kept Edwardian residence located directly opposite the Royal Dublin Society Showgrounds, close to the U.S. and British Embassies in Ballsbridge, and within ten minute walk of Ailesbury Road, the home of many other Diplomatic Missions. Merrion Hall is part of Pat Halpin's group of small hotels – Aberdeen Lodge, also in Ballsbridge, and Halpin's Townhouse in Kilkee - and enjoys the same meticulous attention to detail. The bedrooms are beautifully furnished and equipped with all facilities and some have four-poster beds. The suites are just so comfortable, for as well as having large comfortable beds they have spa baths in which to luxuriate and let the feet recover after a hard day's shopping or visiting the sights. Merrion Hall is a real City dream, completely private with secure parking, a major bonus in Dublin, but best of all one can arrive back laden with bags, just waddle into the gloriously furnished drawing room, sink into a comfortable armchair and relax and have a glass of wine to recover. The staff are tremendous and will look after you without being intrusive or in your face. There is an extensive drawing room menu which features many dishes to ward off the pangs of hunger until it is time to go out to Dinner, or the Theatre. Alternatively, if you just want to stay in and relax in your room and watch T.V. without the

hassle of going out at all, you can do so without being hungry. Ballsbridge now has lots of fashionable buzzy restaurants and bars which are a mere stroll away so you can just dump the car.

| Owners | Pat Halpin |
|---|---|
| Address | 54-56 Merrion Road,Ballsbridge ,Dublin 4 |
| Tel / Fax | 01 6681426 /01 6684280 |
| No. Of rooms | 28 |
| Price, Double/Twin | €130-€160 |
| Single: | €90-€125 |
| Family | €160-€190 |
| Dinner | Drawing room Menu available during the day |
| Open | All Year |
| Credit Cards | Visa MC Diner Amex |
| Directions | Opposite RDS |
| Email | merrionhall@iol.ie |
| | www.lucindaosullivan.com/merrionhall |

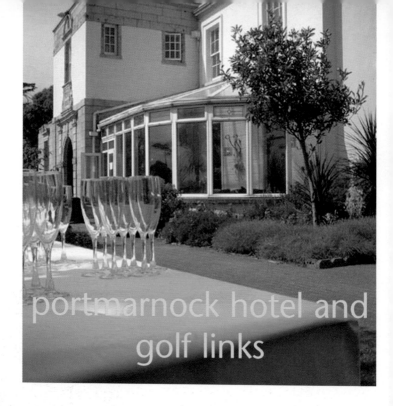

**portmarnock hotel and golf links**

We had driven across from Malahide – one long stretch of horizon, sand, mists, blue, pink and white clouds, broken by jagged rocky islands, all converging in a timeless balmy effervescence of light. Sitting in the Cocktail lounge of the Portmarnock Hotel and Golf Links looking at the magnificent view out across the bay so beautifully captured by the "Irish Impressionist", Walter Osborne, we wondered could it get any better. The house used to belong to the Jameson Whiskey family and was originally known as St. Marnock's. 100 years ago the Jameson family also had a 9 hole golf course and this is now part of their Bernhard Langer designed golf links. Edward V11 often visited the Jameson's and in 1907 unveiled a plaque, created for the occasion of the marriage between two members of the great distilling families, Jameson and Haig. Dinner in the Osborne Room is superb – we had Rock Oysters glazed with champagne and caviar and a hot and cold foie gras followed by Roast Partridge and Challans Duck as the pianist on a Grand Piano played "Someone to Watch Over Me". Try the 7 course Tasting Menu. They also have the more casual Links Restaurant and Bar. Even if you only live in Dublin – Portmarnock seems like a million miles away and it is a fabulous place for a break. For the tourist, it is only 11 miles from the centre of Dublin, yet right on the beach and has a little Moroccan style garden in which to stroll after dinner. It's amazing. Bedrooms are Standard Deluxe which either overlook the sea or the golf course, whilst Executive Rooms all have large bay windows or balconies, three telephones, stereo, CD and video player, minibar, a bathroom scales, 24 hour room service, nightly turndown and concierge service. Children are welcome and babysitters can be arranged. Imagine the pleasure of drinking your Jameson in the Jameson Bar in the former Jameson House now that would really turn my better half on. Shane Cookman runs a great operation.

| | |
|---|---|
| Owners | Shane Cookman (General manager) |
| Address | Strand Road, Portmarnock, Co Dublin |
| Tel / Fax | 01 8460611 /01 8460611 99 |
| No. Of rooms | |
| Price, Double/Twin | From €150 |
| Single: | From €112 |
| Dinner | Yes – 2 Restaurants |
| Open | All Year |
| Credit Cards | All major cards |
| Directions | Easy to find on coast at Portmarnock |

Email
reservations@portmarnock.com
www.lucindaosullivan.com/portmarnockhotel

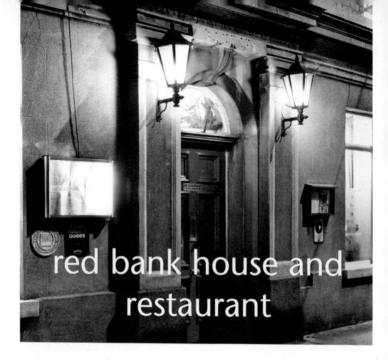

# red bank house and restaurant

### SKERRIES, CO. DUBLIN.

Skerries is a fishing village north of Dublin which is forever in my heart as I spent summers there as a child. It all now seems so simple and real. We would swim on the sandy shore of the south beach be it rain or shine. I still remember being enveloped in a big soft towel and dried off on a wet day whilst the aroma of the frying chips and salt were blown down the beach. My mother would buy prawns from the fishermen while my father slipped into the Stoop Your Head or Joe May's for a pint and a half one which is the colloquialism for a Pint of Guinness and a whiskey. Daddy would then have a smile on his chops while Mother and I would drop the live prawns into the boiling pot for a whisker of a second, take them out and eat them with salt. The local Cinema heralded the delights of Lilac Time with Anna Neagle warbling "we'll gather lilacs in the spring again" … it was a hundred years old then and it seems like a thousand years old now … but Skerries at its heart still retains a wonderful untouched sense of the real Ireland for it is largely undiscovered by tourists.

### RED BANK HOUSE & RESTAURANT

Red Bank House is owned and run by one of Ireland's best-known Chef's, Terry McCoy. Terry is a familiar figure on the Irish foodie scene, not just because he is a striking figure who sports a ponytail and beard but, because he wins awards all round him for his

handling of very fine seafood caught off the Fingal coast. Whilst the Red Bank Restaurant has been a destination Restaurant for the past 20 years or so, it is only in the past couple of years that Terry and Margaret have added 18 rooms by way of the Old Bank House beside the Restaurant and nearby The Red Bank Lodge. The rooms are comfortably furnished, with all mod cons and comforts, in cool nautical colours, blues, yellows and cream but with warmth of feeling. All have T.V. and Internet access. This is a house too for the Gourmet Golfer, for there are forty golf courses within "a driver and a sand wedge" of Skerries and what is better after a quick one at the 19th hole than to come back to enjoy Terry's hospitality and fabulous treatment of our wonderful Dublin Bay Prawns and other seafood. Try the Razor fish, caught locally, which are mainly exported to Japan and, also, ask the see the wine cellar in the old Bank Vault. The Red Bank's long Sunday lunches are legendary. St. Patrick who drove the snakes out of Ireland lived on Church Island off Skerries and fed himself on goat's milk and goat's cheese so you see chevre was popular in Skerries before anywhere else in Ireland. Skerries is only 18 miles from Dublin easily commutable by train and is only 20 minutes drive from Dublin Airport. Walk the beaches, feel the seabreeze in your hair and the sand between your toes, chill out, it is the place.

| | |
|---|---|
| Owners | Terry Mc Coy |
| Address | 5-7 Church Street, Skerries ,Co Dublin |
| Tel / Fax | 01 8491005 /01 8491598 |
| No. Of rooms | 18 |
| Price, Double: | €120 |
| Single: | € 70 |
| Large room | €70 €25 per extra person |
| Dinner | Yes - Restaurant |
| Open | All Year |
| | Restaurant closed for Dinner Sunday nights, 24th and 25th 26th December |
| Credit Cards | All major cards |
| Directions | Opposite AIB Skerries |
| Email | redbank@eircom.net |
| | www.lucindaosullivan.com/redbank |

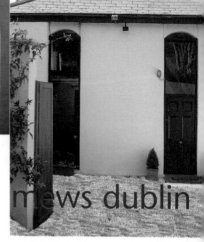

# drummond mews dublin

**L**ooking for that perfect little pied a terre hide away for a stay in Dublin, well Drummond Mews is it. Located in Dublin's exclusive Monkstown, close to the sea, yacht clubs, the fashionable Restaurants of Monkstown, Blackrock, Dun Laoire and Dalkey, Drummond Mews is an original coach house mews to a large Victorian house. Drummond Mews is beside Dun Laoire Golf Club and close to many others. Totally independent and secluded, Drummond Mews has its own private high-walled secure drive in courtyard, where one can dine al fresco, take the sun or just sit and hear the birds sing. The bedroom is very prettily furnished and decorated with Farrow & Ball colours, bathroom en-suite (wash-basin, w.c. and bath). Downstairs has a large Mediterranean style tiled living cum dining room with small kitchen off. Fully equipped with microwave, washerdryer, satellite.t.v. Bedlinen and towels are supplied free of charge. Dublin Tourism 3 star graded. Ten minutes walk to the DART station, which whisks you into central Dublin in 15 minutes.

| | |
|---|---|
| Owners | Mary O'Sullivan |
| Address | |
| Tel / Fax | 01 2800419 |
| No. Of rooms | Mews House Sleeps 2 |
| Price: | €595 - €625 per week |
| Dinner | Self catering |
| Open | All year |
| Credit Cards | Visa.M.C. |
| Directions | Phone above |
| Email | info@dublin-accommodation.net |
| | www.lucindaosullivan.com/drummondmews |

# county galway

As a county, Galway encompasses a University City, the wild splendour and magnificence of Connemara and the Twelve Bens then, to cap it all, you have the Aran Islands. Galway City has a vibrancy all of its own and straddles the Corrib river which thunders down under the Salmon Weir Bridge and winds itself around the City to the lively pedestrianised Quay Street at Wolfe Tone Bridge, where the river enters the famous Galway Bay. Worth seeing is the Spanish Arch, a 16th century structure used to protect galleons unloading wine and rum – most important - and the Collegiate Church of St. Nicholas of Myra, the largest mediaeval church in Ireland, built in 1320 dedicated to the patron saint of sailors. It is almost impossible to find a bed in Galway during Race Week, the Arts Festival, and the Oyster Festival at Clarinbridge so book early. The City abounds with Art Galleries and here you can also visit the home of Nora Barnacle, wife of James Joyce, which is now a small museum. Beyond the Claddagh village from which originated the Claddagh ring – is Salthill – the more honky tonk holiday area with amusement arcades. Moving west around the coast road you come to An Spideal or Spiddle, the heart of the Gaeltacht. Inland is Oughterard, a long pretty village on the River Owenriff, which is very popular with anglers. Oughterard is the gateway to Connemara but a wonderful base for a holiday or break for those who want to have easy access to Galway City. Clifden is the capital of Connemara and is laid out in a triangle. Small and compact but with wide streets and buildings perched high above the deep estuary of the River Owenglin, Clifden is renowned for its Connemara Pony Show. Many famous Irish artists, Paul Henry, Maurice MacGonigal, Jack Yeats, and Sean Keating, have immortalized Clifden in their paintings. The Alcock & Brown Memorial, which commemorates the first transatlantic flight in 1919, is worth seeing. Ten miles northeast of Clifden is Letterfrack, a 19th century Quaker village and just northwest of that is the magnificent Renvyle peninsula, which has strong literary associations.

"A good holiday is one spent among people whose notions of time are vaguer than yours"
(J.B. Priestly)

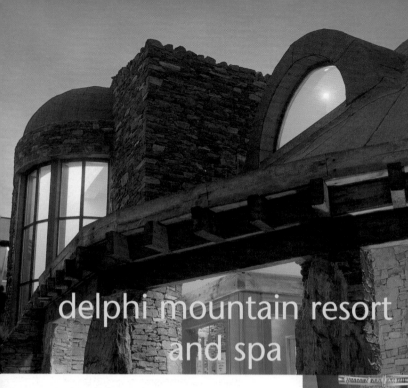

# delphi mountain resort and spa

Set amidst the wild and rugged beauty of the Delphi Valley, on 300 acres of forested estate, Delphi Mountain Resort and Spa is a haven of tranquillity and peace not to be missed. It could only happen in Ireland for Delphi is actually in South Mayo but its postal address is County Galway. Fresh clean unpolluted air, magical scenery, crystal clear water await the visitor. The Lodge, designed to fit into the surrounding landscape, is built in local stone and wood with large bay windows enveloping the scenic beauty. Many bedrooms have patios and Loft Suites are individually themed and decorated in timbers of oak, ash and elm. The dining room serves delicious meals, with organically grown garden vegetables and locally caught fresh fish. There is also a good wine list and a comfortable cocktail bar. The Spa area is superb. Imagine having treatments in a darkened womblike beehive shaped room, as scented candles gently glow and soft relaxing music plays, while a therapist devotes herself to your needs, be it treatments for the face, body or feet, with a range of massage - Aromatherapy,

Swedish, Sports, Reflexology, or Indian Head Massage. Body wraps using seaweed extracts and marine clay are very popular, body exfoliation rids dead skin cells, balneotherapy treatments detox, and anti-cellulite treatments help rid the body of toxins and orange-peel skin. Enjoy the spectacular views of the Mweelrea mountain range with its dramatic snow capped tips, from the large bubbling Jacuzzi with overhead twinkling stars. No wonder this has been voted one of

the top 10 spas in the world by Conde Nast and was the winner of the 2003 Irish Beauty Industry awards. For those who want an active holiday as well as relaxing time, there is The Great Outdoors Option, where walking either power or hill walking, biking, kayaking, canoeing hiking strength training Tai Chi or yoga, surfing, pony trekking, sailing, high ropes course, are all available during your stay. We cycled into Leenane, passing the areas where The Quiet Man was filmed and took a boat trip along Kilary Harbour, the only fjord in Ireland. Otters, Cormorants, wild duck and herons are seen in abundance as well as dolphin watching trips. Magical.

| | | | | | |
|---|---|---|---|---|---|
| Owners | Pat Shaughnessy |
| Address | Leenane, Co. Galway |
| Tel / Fax | 095 42208 /095 42303 |
| No. Of rooms | 22 |
| Price, Double: | €290 |
| Single: | €180 |
| Dinner | Yes |
| Open | January 8th – December 8th |
| Credit Cards | Visa, MC, Diners, Amex |
| Directions | Take N59 to Leenane then it is 7 miles to Delphi |
| Email | delphigy@iol.ie |
| | www.lucindaosullivan.com/delphimountainresort |

# The Galway Radisson
## SAS Hotel and Spa

The Galway Radisson SAS Hotel and Spa is, to the Hotel Industry, what the Lamborghini is to the Motor biz! Sleek in design, powerful in body, the Galway Radisson just purrs. Established in 2001, this 4 Star hotel is only five minutes walk from Eyre Square but boasts fabulous views of Lough Atalia and Galway Bay. The magnificent glass Atrium of the hotel's foyer sets the scene of lightness and clarity within. The stylish Atrium Bar and Lounge with tinkling piano opens out onto a heated terrace where you can have a drink and watch "the sun go down on Galway Bay". The rooms are pretty fab – 217 in total - in various categories and with three room styles: Maritime, Scandinavian, or Classic. Smoking rooms are available, along with Standard, Superior, Business Class, Junior Suites, Executive Suites and Rooms catering for people with a disability. All rooms have a Power Tower, a space saving device that offers satellite television with movie channels, coffee/tea-maker, minibar, and personal safe … whilst the Executive Suites represent the world's highest technological standards. If you really want to splash out Level 5 is top drawer – where Guests are guaranteed privacy and personal service in 16 spacious luxurious executive rooms. Included in Level 5 is a Club Lounge, complimentary treats served throughout the day, soft drinks and canapés during Club Hour, secure membership only access, panoramic rooftop terrace, free use of

the Business Service Centre and a separate meeting room… The stylish split level 220 seater Restaurant Marina is a vision of blue, integrated with dark walnut, reflecting the nautical theme and, as Galway is famous for its seafood, that is the specialty -Galway Bay Oysters, Scallops, Lobster, Monkfish – but there are carnivorous options. Chill out in the Spirit One Spa with facilities found only in the best destination Spas in the world - Sabia Med, Hammam, Rocksauna, Aroma Grotto, Tropical Rain Shower, Cold fog Showers, Ice Drench and Heated Loungers. The Leisure Centre's Swimming Pool is fab along with children's Pool, Jacuzzi, Sauna, Outdoor Canadian Hot Tub Radisson Galway is fantastic.

| Owners | Michael De Haast, General Manager. |
|---|---|
| Address | Lough Atalia Road ,Galway |
| Tel / Fax | 091 538300 /091 538380 |
| No. Of rooms | 217 |
| Price Double/Twin | From €150 |
| Single: | From €130 |
| Family | From €200 |
| Dinner | Yes - Restaurant |
| Open | All Year |
| Credit Cards | All major Cards |
| Directions | 5 minutes from Eyre Square on Lough Atalia waterfront |

Email
reservations.galway@radissonsas.com
www.lucindaosullivan.com/galwayradisson

iverna cottage

**M**any emigrants have the idea of coming home, building a little cottage in the West and living happily ever after. Very many never get to live out their dream but this is exactly what Patricia and Willie Farrell have done – and what a cottage and what a happy ending. They are delightful people, big hearted, warm and friendly, who love books, a glass of wine, and company. They have built the most delicious cottage using wood, slate and stone, encircled by flowers and with the view over Galway Bay – it is pure heaven. Although newly built there is a feeling of the old world with antiques, lovely rugs, paintings, and other old Irish artifacts, around the house. Patricia and Willie will welcome you with refreshments in their sitting room and make you feel at home. Iverna is an ideal base for trips further west and for visiting the Bookshops, Galleries, and sights of Galway City. Every lane leads to the beach and resident dog, Cossa, likes to go along with you.
Every road leads to a pub or a restaurant where

you can have dinner before returning to the comfort of Iverna. The four bedrooms have restored cast-iron bedsteads and handmade patchwork or quilted bedspreads and are extremely comfortable with all facilities. Sit in the dingly dell wildflower garden with large rockery and bridged stream and contemplate

the state of the Nation – hopefully with a glass in hand. Willie gets to squeeze the orange juice every morning – keep him at it. Patricia prepares a fresh fruit cup in pretty fluted glass compotes and, not only are they in pretty glasses but, the fruit is marinated in liqueur before being drizzled with Irish honey and yogurt. There are cereals galore and then you can have the Full Irish – with scrummy potato cake – or French toast and bacon – or kippers on request along with homemade bread, scones, muffins or croissants. Patricia very obligingly will cater for any dietary requirements, with advance notice of course. Children are welcome, with one-third discount, and there are two family rooms. I think I'll move in.

| Owners | Patricia and William Farrell |
|---|---|
| Address | Salahoona, Spiddal, Co Galway |
| Tel / Fax | 091 553762 |
| No. Of rooms | 4 |
| Price, Double: | €70-€80 |
| Single: | Supplement |
| Dinner | No |
| Open | April1st – October 31st |
| Credit Cards | None |
| Directions | Signposted in Spiddal village |
| Email | ivernacottage@ireland.com |
| | www.lucindaosullivan.com/ivernacottage |

# joyces waterloo house

**M**y better half, Brendan likes to book in advance and feel secure in that he will have a bed for the night. I, on the other hand, much prefer to take off and see what I will find. Very often about 6 o'clock, with not a sign of a bed being secured, he gets really narky as I keep on saying- "you never know what is around the corner". That is how I found Joyce's Waterloo House on the edge of Clifden, Co. Galway.

Patricia and P.K. Joyce are a young couple with energetic, enthusiastic ideas, which is clear from their terrific Waterloo House. Waterloo is one of the new breed of Guesthouses which provides a Hotel service in beautiful surroundings. The bedrooms are spacious and stylishly decorated and you can even enjoy your breakfast in bed. Superior rooms have King-size beds, sofas, and walk-on balconies overlooking fabulous Connemara. Rooms to the rear have 4 poster beds whilst Standard rooms have a mixture of regular, double beds and Kingsize beds – so ask when booking. Bedrooms have various extras in situ - T.V. VCR, beverage trays,

magazines, spring water, and power showers. Patricia's Dinner menu (book before 13.00 hours) is all freshly cooked from local produce including smoked salmon salad, steaks, poached or grilled salmon, Connemara lamb Irish stew. Vegans are well catered for too. After dinner you might consider a real Irish Coffee or a spell in their Outdoor Hot Tub under the stars. Alternatively, there are lots of Restaurants in Clifden (15 minutes walk) and Patricia or P.K. will happily drop you in and you can get a taxi back out. After a blissful night's sleep in the peace of Connemara, you can look forward to a great breakfast with the Famous Connemara Fry, poached eggs with smoked salmon or bacon, or a ham cheese and fresh fruit plate, along with an eclectic selection of teas and coffees from Earl Grey through Starbucks – and not forgetting their fruit infusions and hot chocolate drinks. This should set you up for the scubadiving or whatever is your fancy for the day.

| Owners | Patricia and P.K Joyce |
|---|---|
| Address | Galway Road , Clifden, Co Galway |
| Tel / Fax | 095 21688 /095 22044 |
| No. Of rooms | 8 |
| Price, Double: | €114 |
| Single: | €76 |
| Dinner | Yes - BYO Wine |
| Open | All Year |
| Credit Cards | Visa MC Amex Diners Laser |
| Directions | Sign posted on road into Clifden from Galway |
| Email | pkp@joyces-waterloo.com |
| | www.lucindaosullivan.com/joyceswaterloohouse |

# renvyle house hotel

"My house…stands on a lake, but it stands also on the sea – waterlillies meet the golden seaweed. It is as if, in the faery land of Connemara at the extreme end of Europe, the incongruous flowed together at last, and the sweet and bitter blended. Behind me, islands and mountainous mainland share in a final reconciliation, at this, the world's end". So wrote Oliver St. John Gogarty in 1927 of his then home. Spectacularly located nestling between the blue Twelve Bens mountain range and the Shores of the Atlantic Ocean, Renvyle has a tremendous history and it has always attracted famous people from all over the world. The house has been pulled down, rebuilt, burnt to ashes, rebuilt again. It has been home to Donal O'Flaherty, Chieftan of one of the oldest and most powerful Clans of Connaught, and to Mrs. Caroline Blake who was the first to open it as a hotel way back in 1883. But, enough of the past, for Renvyle has been a hotel for all seasons and has always moved with the times and now in 2004 is a stylish destination which is hugely popular with the Irish public, who return again and again for blissful respite and evenings filled with fun. Situated on 200 acres, Renvyle has a lake teaming with trout, a heated outdoor pool, a 9 hole golf course and their own beach. There is clay pigeon shooting, horse riding in season, buckets of activities and creche facilities during holiday periods. Pets are allowed "within reason" – enquire - for that doesn't mean Pooch can sit up with his Cartier collar at the dining table! Throughout the year there are Painting Breaks, Murder Mystery Weekends, Fly Fishing instruction, Golf Breaks and Walking Breaks. Sixty- eight bedrooms, five suites, are spacious and very comfortable with all that even the most difficult guest could possibly desire. Excellent food is based on fresh local produce, Connemara lamb, game, fresh fish. In fact Renvyle Chef, Tim O'Sullivan, won the annual Moreau Chablis fish cookery competition in 2003. Classical Pianist, Derek Hoffman, accompanies dinner each evening, on Count John McCormack's Steinway Grand Piano – playing it that is! Oh, I want to get in the car and drive there again this minute … Ronnie Counihan runs a great house.

| Owners | Ronnie Counihan (Chief Executive) |
| --- | --- |
| Address | Renvyle, Connemara, Co Galway |
| Tel / Fax | 095 43511 /095 43515 |
| No. Of rooms | 68 |
| Price, Double: | From €120 |
| Single: | From €60 |
| Dinner | Yes |
| Open | February – January |
| Credit Cards | All major cards accepted |
| Directions | Take N59 from Galway to Renvyle Hotel signed in Village |

Email        info@renvyle.com
www.lucindaosullivan.com/renvylehouse

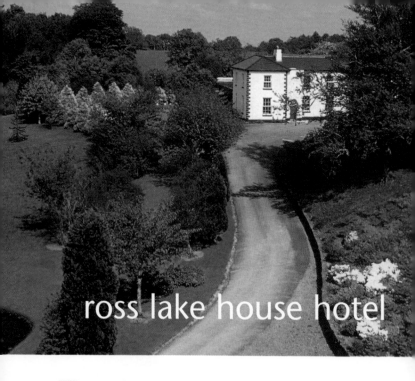

# ross lake house hotel

Fancy waking up in a four poster bed in a splendid Georgian house, on 6 acres of rambling woods and rolling lawns, in the magnificent wilderness of Connemara, then Henry and Elaine Reid's Ross Lake House Hotel is for you. Ross Lake House was formerly part of the Killaguile estate built by James Edward Jackson, land agent for Lord Iveagh at Ashford Castle, but renamed as a Country House Hotel because of its proximity to Ross Lake and the fishing waters of Lough Corrib. With 13 spacious guestrooms and suites, all beautifully and individually designed to reflect the charm and graciousness of the house, yet provide the modern facilities we all expect nowadays, you will be very comfortable. There are lovely classic rooms oozing with country house charm, fabulous superior rooms with period furniture and luxurious fabrics, and then, stunning suites with own sitting area. As pretty Oughterard is only 22 km from Galway City it is ideal for visiting the vibrancy that is Galway but choosing to leave it when you wish. There are Golf Courses all round – Oughterard, Barna, Galway Bay and Ballyconneely Links Course so if he wants to swing a club you can take off to the Antique shops. You are also ideally poised at Ross Lake for doing the rugged wilder aspects of the Connemara of "The Quiet Man". There is a cosy library bar to snuggle into and a delightful drawingroom

with blazing fires. The dining room is elegant and the Chef concentrates on the finest fresh produce from the Connemara hills, rivers, lakes and the Atlantic ocean. Henry and Elaine are charming and helpful hosts and, believe me, you will really enjoy a spell at their lovely Ross Lake House.

| | |
|---|---|
| Owners | Henry and Elaine Reid |
| Address | Rosscahill, Oughterard ,Co Galway |
| Tel / Fax | 091 550109 /091 550184 |
| No. Of rooms | 13 |
| Price, Double: | €150-€170 |
| Single: | Single Supplement €30 |
| | 50% reduction for children sharing |
| Dinner | Yes |
| Open | March15th – October 31st |
| Credit Cards | All major cards |
| Directions | Follow N59 towards Clifden Hotel signposted after Moycullen |
| Email | rosslake@iol.ie |
| | www.lucindaosullivan.com/rosslakehousehotel |

# county kerry

Co. Kerry is known as "the Kingdom" and it is difficult to know where one starts to list the attractions of this amazing area. There is the world famous Killarney with its three lakes and impressive McGillycuddy Reeks looming behind them with their ever changing shades and colours. Almost as well known is the hair raising and breathtaking Ring of Kerry on the Iveragh peninsula with its sheer drops and stark coastal scenery. Coaches are required to travel anti-clockwise and leave Killarney between 10 and 11 a.m. so if you are doing it in a day, you need to be earlier or you will be behind them all day. Some books tell you to drive clockwise but it can be nerve racking if you meet a coach on a narrow pass as I have experienced. Head out to Killorglin famous for its mid-August Puck Fair where eating, drinking, dancing, singing is reigned over by the King of the Festival, a Puck Goat. From Killorglin move on taking in the beautiful Caragh Lake to Glenbeigh with Rossbeigh's sweeping beach. On to Cahersiveen and swing out via the new bridge to Valentia island. Come back

"A folk song is a song nobody ever wrote" (anon)

and head south to Waterville where Charlie Chaplin and family spent their summers. The final stage is Caherdaniel to Sneem and the lush subtropical richness of Parknasilla which is then about eighteen miles from the popular town of Kenmare. North of the county is Listowel famous for its Writers Week and generally regarded as the literary capital of Ireland but also celebrates a madly popular Horse Race Week. Tralee, the principal town of the county, is a very busy commercial centre and also hosts the famous Rose of Tralee celebration. Dingle of "Ryan's Daughter" fame is stunning and has a life of its own. It also has Fungi the dolphin. Among Kerry's many famous Championship Golf Courses is Ballybunion, the favourite haunt of American golfer, Tom Watson, who was once captain of the famous Club. Kerry has an abundance of eateries at all prices and in keeping with Irish tradition is well catered for in drinking establishments, many of which provide ballads and folk songs.

# aghadoe heights hotel

A ghadoe Heights Hotel at Killarney is not just any ordinary Hotel it is an experience. 5 star unpretentious luxury at your fingertips, just the right distance outside the centre of the Town and overlooking the Killarney Lakes. The Aghadoe Heights is bliss and switch off time, from which you will only be disturbed by solicitous and gentle pampering by the ever attentive staff. The public rooms are furnished with a mélange of elegant eclectic pieces from the Far East, mixed through with French antiques, fine paintings and sculptures. Luxurious elegant bedrooms have balconies and bathrooms which have a Zen like feel. A Roman style indoor swimming pool is rather originally placed to the front of the building so, as you swim, you can still see the lakes and mountains with their ever changing palette of moody colours. Right next door to the pool is a snug little bar which appeals to the men whilst you slip upstairs to the open plan lounge and have the most scrumptious afternoon tea served by white gloved girls or you could spend time in the Beauty Rooms. I would go to the Aghadoe Heights for the afternoon tea alone – and people do. Frederick's Restaurant is incorporated in this large first floor open plan area and while you eat the most delicious food a pianist is playing away on the grand piano. The menu might have lobster or smoked fillet of venison with fresh linguine, juniper and orange jus and on a Sunday people drive up to one hundred miles for the spectacularly lavish Sunday Lunch Buffet. Bliss and even more bliss

for, as we go to press, Aghadoe
Heights are adding on 22
magnificent suites and the most
fabulous Destination Spa ever -
book your helicopter space.
Chauffeur service to and from
Kerry Airport available.

| | |
|---|---|
| Owners | Pat and Marie Chawke (General Managers) |
| Address | Lakes of Killarney, Co Kerry, Ireland |
| Tel / Fax | 064 31766 / 064 31345 |
| No. Of rooms | 75 |
| Price, Double: | €200-€700 |
| Single: | €200 |
| Dinner | Restaurant A la Carte Menu/Lounge Menu |
| Open | March – December inclusive |
| Credit Cards | All major Cards |
| Directions | 2 miles, west of Killarney sign posted off N22 |
| Email | info@aghadoeheights.com |
| | www.lucindaosullivan.com/aghadoeheightshotel |

*carrig country house and restaurant*

Caragh Lake is a lush magnificent area virtually hidden away from the Tourist be they Irish or otherwise. It has however been a popular area for many years with the Germans a number of whom bought houses in the 1960's.

## CARRIG HOUSE

We discovered Carrig House, an original 19th C. hunting lodge, at Caragh Lake in 1997 quite by accident when we arrived out there disheveled and distraught with two young boys on tow. We were staying in a dreadful B. & B. in Killorglin which had thimbles of watery orange juice and brown physchedelic sheets from the 1970's and we nearly cried when we realized we could have been in luxury in Carrig House had we but known of it. We couldn't find anywhere to eat in Killorglin and were at one another's throats when a young girl told us about "the new house out at the lake". Off we took like the clappers, 4 miles out of Killorglin, to find there was a God, and Heaven awaited in the shape of Frank Slattery, and his wife Mary, who had opened for business that summer. Even if we couldn't stay there on that occasion at least we were able to have dinner in the magnificent William Morris papered diningroom overlooking the mysterious lake with its

mountainous background. We did however return again and it was as blissful as we had first thought. Arthur Rose Vincent chose Carrig House in which to live after his former residence, Muckross Estate in Killarney, was made over to the Irish State by his American father in law, following the death of his young wife. Arthur clearly had an eye for beauty. The 4 acres of gardens have 935 different species of mature trees and plants, including some very rare and exotic varieties, and are just divine. Dingly dell, mixes with rolling lawns sweeping down to the private jetty which has boats for fishing or just for guests' pleasure. Splendid new rooms have been added at Carrig including a Presidential Suite. The food is great and Frank and Mary, while professional to their fingertips, are just fun. People relax and there is laughter and buzz at Carrig. We had torn ourselves reluctantly away and as we drove out the gates My Beloved surprisingly broke into verse "I come from haunts of coot and hern, I make a sudden sally …"

| | |
|---|---|
| Owners | Frank and Mary Slattery |
| Address | Caragh Lake,Killorglin ,Co Kerry,Ireland |
| Tel / Fax | 066 9769100  /066 9769166 |
| No. Of rooms | 16 |
| Price, Double: | €120-€350 |
| Single: | Single supplement €50 not applicable to suites |
| | Extra bed in room per person €35 |
| Dinner | Restaurant |
| Open | March 3rd-December 6th |
| Credit Cards | Visa MC Diners |
| Directions | Left after 2.5 miles on N70 Killorglin –Glenbeigh Road (Ring of Kerry) |
| Email | info@carrighouse.com www.lucindaosullivan.com/carrighouse |

# Glanleam country house and gardens

Glanleam House and estate is undoubtedly Paradise in Ireland complete with its own Rain Forest – jungle. Situated on Valentia Island, (now linked to the mainland by a bridge), Glanleam House dates from the early 19th Century and was originally home to the Knight of Kerry. Magnificently and stylishly furnished to the very highest standard, blending the best of antique and modern furniture and design, it really is superb. The six bedrooms and one suite are cool and comfortable with beautiful views of the garden and water. Valentia is Europe's most westerly harbour with nothing but ocean between it and Newfoundland. The island also basks in the Gulf Stream climate and is an oasis of sub-tropical plants, ferns, myrtle, bamboos and the only remaining camphor tree in the British Isles. It was from Valentia Island that the first ever trans-Atlantic telegraph cable was laid and for years it was said there was better communication between Valentia and New York than Valentia and Dublin! In 1992 the oldest fossilized footprints in the northern hemisphere were discovered, nearly 400 million years old, and belonging to a marine tetrapod that pre-dated the dinosaurs. You needn't worry about dinosaurs, however, just enjoy the lovely rare Soay sheep and Connemara ponies living happily in this blissful haven. Dinner is available 5 nights a week with advance notice so do enquire on booking. Meta Kreissig offers both Irish and German cuisine with fruit and vegetables from their own walled Victorian gardens. Superb local fresh fish, meat and poultry, feature and you can be assured that you will be admirably looked after at beautiful Glanleam. From here too you can arrange to visit the spectacular Skelligs Rocks. Deep sea, shore and lake fishing, watersports, hill walking and horseriding are all available locally. Golfers will find Waterville Golf Links an attraction.

| Owners | Meta Kreissig |
|---|---|
| Address | Glanleam Estate, Valentia Island, Co Kerry |
| Tel / Fax | 066 9476176 /066 9476108 |
| No. Of rooms | 7 |
| Price, Double: Single: | €140-€260 |
| Dinner | Yes – 5 nights |
| Open | March 17th – October 31. |
| Credit Cards | Visa MC Amex |
| Directions | Take R565 through Portmagee to Valentia Island House signed |

Email      info@glanleam.com
www.lucindaosullivan.com/glanleam

# great southern hotel killarney

The first time I was in Killarney was many years ago with a gang of girls for the Circuit of Ireland Rally. We weren't really interested in the Rally, more in what was driving the cars! People congregated in the Bar in the Great Southern Hotel and I was mesmerized by how beautiful it was, for we were staying in a B. & B. with pink nylon sheets and doubtful towels. That is all a long time ago.

The Great Southern Hotel is one of the Grand Old Ladies of the Irish Hospitality scene and, very recently, she has not just had Botox but a major face-lift, returning her to the ranks she deserves as one of the finest Hotels in Ireland. Presidents and Princes have been entertained at the GSH Killarney and there is a very definite feeling of regal splendour from the moment you approach the impressive pillared entrance, go up the steps and know that you are somewhere special. The Hotel is fabulously located close to the old world Railway Station and, if you use your imagination a little, you can just see the Victorian ladies in hoop dresses alighting from the train and walking across to the Hotel with bearers in tow carrying stacks of trunks. Although the Hotel is in the centre of Killarney it is on 20 acres of secluded landscaped gardens in an amazing setting. The bedrooms are spacious and elegant with high ceilings and facilities for modem, fax and email along with a minibar, T.V. and radio. Luxury Suites have been individually designed to re-create an old world ambience and some have chandeliers and separate dressing rooms. There are two dining options. The Garden Restaurant is fabulous with its high domed ceiling and gracious ambience – look up and wonder just how much gold leaf was used to restore this room to its present magnificence. Peppers is the Hotel's more casual Bistro style

Restaurant very handy if you want something less formal. The Innisfallen Spa at the Southern has a wide range of facilities so that you can be totally pampered – try the Hydro-massage baths they are brilliant, followed by a Monsoon Shower

| | |
|---|---|
| Owners | Conor Hennigan (General Manager ) |
| Address | Town Centre, Killarney, Co Kerry. |
| Tel / Fax | 064 38000 /064 35300 |
| No. Of rooms | 172 |
| Price, Double: | €230-€250 |
| Single: | €230-€250 |
| Dinner | Yes – 2 Restaurants |
| Open | All year |
| Credit Cards | Visa MC Diners Amex |
| Directions | Located on the Square in Killarney town |
| Email | res@killarney-gsh.com |

www.lucindaosullivan.com/gshkillarney

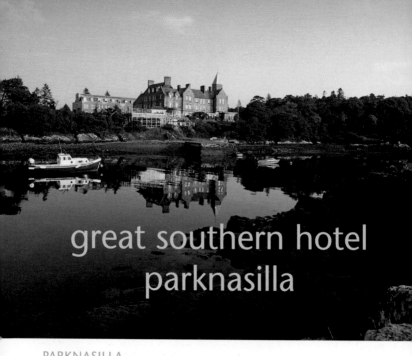

# great southern hotel parknasilla

### PARKNASILLA

I always insist that we set off a day in advance when we are going to the Great Southern at Parknasilla because, I just love it so much I want to arrive in a civilized state, and not be below par for one minute. We break the back of the journey by staying somewhere reasonably priced and reasonably close. Next morning refreshed and ready to make our entrance we take a leisurely drive out through Cahirciveen, around the Ring of Kerry, absolutely reveling in just being alive and being in the spectacular scenery that is the Ring of Kerry. Brave souls, and we were those soldiers one year, can drive from Caragh Lake out over the McGillicuddy Reeks past mountainy rangy goats and hair-rising roads emerging down close to Sneem.

### GREAT SOUTHERN HOTEL PARKNASILLA

The Great Southern Hotel at Parknasilla is the jewel in the crown of the Great Southern Hotel Group sitting majestically in 300 acres of the most beautiful lush sub-tropical parkland overlooking Kenmare Bay. It is probably the most splendid Hotel in the country, in the sense of location and Victorian Grandeeism. In the old days it was a railway Hotel and people were

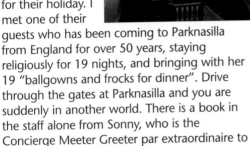

picked up from Kenmare station and conveyed in state to Parknasilla for their holiday. I met one of their guests who has been coming to Parknasilla from England for over 50 years, staying religiously for 19 nights, and bringing with her 19 "ballgowns and frocks for dinner". Drive through the gates at Parknasilla and you are suddenly in another world. There is a book in the staff alone from Sonny, who is the Concierge Meeter Greeter par extraordinaire to beat all par extraordinaires, to Head Porter Michael and Jackie the Maitre d' of the dining room. These are the smoothest most accomplished men at their trades that you are likely to meet anywhere in the world – Masters at their Arts – and greet you as though you were the most important person ever, a long lost friend, and will look after you likewise. The bedrooms are spacious and comfortable and for me a great switch off point. Look out front and people will be sitting around on the terrace sipping cool drinks or walking the grounds. There is a 12 Hole Golf Course and Horseriding, anything can be organized along with trips around the rugged inlets on the Parknasilla Princess. The dining room is vast and yet the food does not suffer from its size. Retire to the Library, view the wonderful art collection, swim in the pool, luxuriate in the Canadian Outdoor Hot tub, take part in the walks or activities organized, get totally tiddily, dance the mambo after dinner to the band, nobody will bat an eyelid, certainly not the General Manager, Jim Feeney, who steers this great ship with impeccable precision and has seen it all!

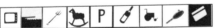

| Owners | Jim Feeney (General Manager) |
| --- | --- |
| Address | Parknasilla, Sneem, Co. Kerry. |
| Tel / Fax | 064 45122 /064 45323 |
| No. Of rooms | 83 |
| Price, Double: | From €260.  Family (2A+2C) From €360. Plus special packages BBD |
| Dinner | 2 Restaurants |
| Open | All Year |
| Credit Cards | All Major Cards |
| Directions | N70 from Kenmare – Estate entrance after Tahilla just before Sneem Village. |
| Email | res@parknasilla-gsh.com |
| | www.lucindaosullivan.com/gshparknasilla |

# greenmount house

## DINGLE

The Dingle peninsula is so intensely shatteringly beautiful that one can almost feel its raging tempestuous undercurrent churning away. The movie "Ryan's Daughter" brought people from all over the world to Dingle and they still come in their droves. Apart from the amazing scenery, the Dingle peninsula has one of the greatest concentrations of Celtic ruins, Ringforts, Beehives and stone crosses. People come too to see Fungi the dolphin, who is undoubtedly Dingle's most famous resident. Worth seeing also are the Harry Clarke stained glass windows in the former Presentation Convent in Green Street. There are lots of Restaurants in Dingle Town, which used to be an old Spanish trading Port, notably Jim McCarthy's Chart House for Jim is the consummate host. Try also Out of the Blue opposite the Tourist Office, which has outside tables and does very reasonable seafood.

## GREENMOUNT HOUSE

That John and Mary Curran's Greenmount House is one of the best known Guest Houses in Dingle is down to the fact that John and Mary made it so themselves. Accolades and Awards do not come without very hard work in any business and John and Mary have been providing the best of luxury accommodation and breakfasts for over 20 years. Both are from old Dingle families and there isn't a stick or stone on the peninsula that they don't know about. It is a relaxed friendly house and you will feel comfortable and welcome there. Being only 200 yards stroll to

the centre of Dingle town you can dump the car and paddle home after dinner in any of the many Restaurants. Greenmount has been extended over the years and is now in two parts linked by a long Conservatory diningroom, which is lovely in both winter and summer. Superior rooms are split level and stylish, suites really, with large seating areas. All are furnished and decorated to the highest standards, with direct dial phones and T.V. and doors that lead out to a balcony, from which the elevated view of Dingle Harbour can be enjoyed while sipping a glass of something special after a hard days enjoyment! Breakfasts served in the conservatory are legendary with a wonderful selection of fresh and poached fruits, cereals, cheeses, homemade preserves, and breads before you then tackle into the hot variety. Children over 7 welcome. All the "wannabe" awards have been won – what more would many do but sit back and gloat – but not the Currans they are still dedicated to maintaining the standards they set themselves.

| | |
|---|---|
| Owners | John and Mary Curran |
| Address | Dingle, Co Kerry |
| Tel / Fax | 066 9151414 /066 9151974 |
| No. Of rooms | 11 |
| Price, Double: | €100-€140 |
| Family | €150 per room |
| Dinner | No |
| Open | All Year |
| Credit Cards | Visa ,MC |
| Directions | Go up John St. continue up hill to Greenmount on left |
| Email | greenmounthouse@eircom.net |
| | www.lucindaosullivan.com/greenmounthouse |

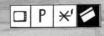

# heatons guest house

We had intended setting off for Dingle early in the morning but we fell by the wayside. We had stayed at a house up at Caragh Lake, demurely had dinner beside an American couple without exchanging a word, walked around the house and came back in to the drawingroom to sit quietly in a bay window. Suddenly the door opened and a bright smiling blonde girl came in sat down and introduced herself as Marian. She and her husband, Nigel, were on their first trip to Ireland as their son was on a school rugby trip in Limerick. As often happens with English people who have no family connections with Ireland, it was their first trip here, and frankly they wouldn't have come unless they had to, for they usually went to exotic locations all over the world. We had a drink, and another drink before Nigel sensibly suggested they retire. Next morning at breakfast we all waved at one another politely, had little polite chats, and nodded to the Americans. We got our bags out to the car, where the American couple were trying to map out their route. Telling us they had Restaurants in the States, I confessed to being probably their archenemy – a Restaurant Critic. With that a German car swung into the car park and having met the Americans earlier came over to the car to join in. On his learning of my occupation over he went to his boot and took out a little fold up table, spread a check cloth, took out two bottles of wine from his region in Germany, some tidbits, special knives and told us he had been coming to Ireland for over 30 years, using the same table, knives and equipment each year! Nigel and Marian emerged and we had the league of nations Irish, English, Americans and Germans, having a party in a car park in Kerry, They had never experienced anything like it and told us since it was the best trip of their lives. That's what Kerry and Ireland is really all about.

## HEATON'S GUESTHOUSE

Cameron and Nuala Heaton's eponymous Guesthouse is spectacularly located on the edge of the water with magnificent views of Dingle Bay. There is something special about being close to the water that is infectious and life giving. The shimmering ripples are wonderful to sit by during the summer and stunningly dramatic viewed through a window in the depths of Winter. Heaton's has 16 rooms, standard, deluxe and junior suites, take your choice, but all are beautifully draped and furnished in cool clear, up to the minute, stylish colours. Each with T.V. Tea/Coffee makers, and superb bathrooms with power-showers, are spacious and have everything you could possibly want for your comfort. There is a large foyer and a lounge sittingroom area with big comfortable sofas where you can snuggle up, cosy up, or just relax. Breakfast is served in the diningroom which also makes the most of the magnificent views with big plate glass windows. This is daughter, Jackie's, area and you can chose from an amazing selection which includes juices, fruits, cereals, stewed fruits – rhubarb or apple- porridge with a dram of Drambuie, brown sugar and cream, followed by the traditional Irish, or catch of the day, local smoked salmon and scrambled egg. Preserves and breads are home-made. Children over 8 welcome. Cameron and Nuala are delightful people, as is their daughter Jackie, and superb hospitality is their middle name.

| | |
|---|---|
| Owners | Cameron and Nuala Heaton |
| Address | The Wood, Dingle ,Co Kerry |
| Tel / Fax | 066 9152288 /066 9152324 |
| No. Of rooms | 16 |
| Price, Double: | €118 |
| Single: | €95 |
| Family Room: | €148 |
| Dinner | No |
| Open | February 6th –January 2nd |
| Credit Cards | Visa MC |
| Directions | Look for Marina - Heatons is about 600 yards beyond it |
| Email | heatons@iol.ie |
| | www.lucindaosullivan.com/heatonsguesthouse |

# muxnaw lodge

Kenmare is one of the major destinations in Kerry. Now a cosmopolitan Town with many Restaurants, Pubs, Art Galleries, Designer Boutiques and Delicatessens, it can be expensive but is definitely a very enjoyable, buzzy, happening town. The drive over the mountains through rock tunnels from Glengarriff in West Cork is spectacular as likewise is the trip from Killarney.

## MUXNAW LODGE
There is a wide variety of accommodation and high prices in Kenmare so finding that something in between can sometimes be difficult. Muxnaw lodge was built in 1801 and is ideally situated close to the town on the Castletownbere Road. Muxnaw is a homely place nestled in fine gardens, complete with its own all weather tennis court, and enjoys outstanding views of The Kenmare River and Suspension Bridge. Tranquil bedrooms are all different, furnished with antiques, and all have tea and coffee making faciletes. Its success is a credit to the wonderful hospitality of its hostess Hannah Boland as well as the comforts provided. Hannah knows the area like the back of her hand and delights in mapping out routes and setting her guests off on the proper track for the day .I have indeed seen her spend many an afternoon, after she served the most delectable afternoon tea, chatting with her guests and pouring over maps and routes mapping the

remainder of their holiday. Kenmare has any number of Restaurants to tickle one's taste buds but sometimes it is preferable to relax at base and enjoy home cooking all done on the big Aga cooker. Dinner must be booked by noon. There is no wine licence so you are welcome to bring your own. Breakfast is also excellent. Hannahs generosity constantly shines through with a fine spread. A very good value spot in a period house in up market Kenmare.

| | |
|---|---|
| Owners | Hannah Boland |
| Address | Castletownbere Road, Kenmare ,Co Kerry |
| Tel / Fax | 064 41252 |
| No. Of rooms | 5 |
| Price, Double: | €70 |
| Single: | |
| Dinner | Yes - book by noon |
| Open | All Year closed 24/25 December |
| Credit Cards | Visa |
| Directions | On Castletownbere Road out of Kenmare |
| Email | muxnawlodge@eircom.net |
| | www.lucindaosullivan.com/muxnawlodge |

# ocean wave country house

N oreen O'Toole's pretty pink house, Ocean Wave, at 1 km away is just the right distance for enjoying all that the village of Glenbeigh has to offer. On the Ring of Kerry, the pretty village of Glenbeigh makes an ideal base for visiting Killarney, Waterville, or for nipping up to Dingle for the day. It is within eight miles of the town of Killorglin where the annual festival of Puck Fair is held where, a Goat is tethered on a platform high above the town and is King of the festival for the week. To the other side is the magnificent Rossbeigh strand, a three-mile stretch on a blue flag beach. Ocean Wave is extremely comfortable and meticulously maintained with lovely luxurious bedrooms each individually draped and furnished with Napoleonic style canopies over the beds, French style chairs, and some even have Jacuzzi baths. Built on a rise, Ocean Wave has wonderful views out over Dingle Bay and Dooks Golf club and its pretty garden, with lush hydrangeas and tropical plants, is just the place to sit and relax on a summer's day, perhaps with a glass of aromatic Gewurztraminer in your hand. From here too you can drive up around Caragh Lake, which is well worth a visit. Noreen

doesn't do dinner but there are plenty of places locally. In the morning you can expect a wonderful breakfast spread – juices, cereals, fresh and dried fruits, and a fine selection of hot breakfasts – potato cakes with bacon or smoked Cromane salmon, the full Irish, grilled kippers, home baked breads and steaming hot tea. You won't be hungry. Ocean Wave is bliss as it is a non-smoking house and offers very comfortable accommodation at a reasonable price.

| | | |
|---|---|---|
| Owners | Nora O Toole | |
| Address | Glenbeigh ,Co Kerry | |
| Tel / Fax | 066 9768249 / 0669768412 | |
| No. Of rooms | 6 | |
| Price, Double/Twin | €80 | |
| Single: | €50 | |
| Dinner | No | |
| Open | March1st – October 31st | |
| Credit Cards | None | |
| Directions | Beside Glenbeigh Village on Ring of Kerry | |
| Email | oceanwave@iol.ie | |
| | www.lucindaosullivan.com/oceanwave | |

# county kilkenny

Kilkenny is a county of rich farmland, quaint villages and towns, well endowed with mediaeval ruins and friendly people who are not reluctant to talk about hurling, the very special Gaelic game at which Kilkenny people excel. Kilkenny City, on the River Nore, is a bustling busy place defined by the magnificent Kilkenny Castle, former home to the Butlers of Ormonde. The City has many hotels, guesthouses and bars and is very popular now for weekend breaks and for stag and hen parties. The surrounding county is not short on items of historical interest like Kilcree Round Tower, Jerpoint Abbey, and the ruin of Kells Priory.  Go to Graiguenamanagh on the River Barrow, the home of Duiske Abbey, founded in 1204, and although much altered over the years the 13th Century interior has been lovingly preserved. Bennettsbridge, an area now home to many craft industries such as the Nicholas Mosse Pottery, is worth a visit, as is Thomastown, just north of Jerpoint, formerly a walled town of some importance, and close to the magnificent Championship Golf Course of Mount Juliet. Relax with a glass of Guinness, or whatever, in the tree lined square, or by the river, of interesting Inistioge, which is overlooked by the ruin of the Woodstock Estate, burned down in 1922.  Kilkenny is a fabulous county.

"I have made an important discovery...that alcohol, taken in sufficient quantities, produces all the effects of intoxication".
(Oscar Wilde)

# belmore

Belmore is a lovely Georgian hunting lodge built in 1790 for the eponymous Earl of Belmore. Superbly located in a prime spot right on the River Nore beside the magnificent Mount Juliet Estate, it is ideal for those wanting the best of both worlds. The aristocracy knew how to look after themselves back then and nothing but the best would do, so this is a super spot. The house is very unusual inside with part vaulted "castle feel" ceilings and from the lovely bedrooms, you can actually see the famous Jack Nicklaus designed golf course at Mount Juliet. Joe and Rita Teesdale are an absolute delight and take pleasure in showing the historical ruined mediaeval village of Newtown Jerpoint with the tomb of St. Nicholas in the graveyard of the church which actually lies on their farmland. Joe is Chairman of the Southern Fisheries Board, which is responsible for river fishing from the Blackwater to the Barrow and, if you are tempted to throw in a line on their stretch of the River Nore game fishing is free for their guests. The yard adjoining the house is a very fine example of a Georgian stableyard. Principally a sheep farm, Joe also grows barley, sugar beet and fodder for local horse owners. Belmore is a demonstration R.E.P.S. (Rural

Environmental Protection Scheme) farm and as such they are attracting endangered species of wildlife including birds such as Goldcrest and plovers. They also have five out of seven native species of Bats on the farm in outbuildings and the ruins. Belmore is ideal for visiting Kilkenny Castle and City for it is only 30 minutes away as well as being at the centre of the Kilkenny Craft Trail.

| | |
|---|---|
| Owners | Joseph and Rita Teesdale |
| Address | Belmore ,Jerpoint Church,Thomastown , Co Kilkenny. |
| Tel / Fax | 056 7724228 /None |
| No. Of rooms | 3 |
| Price, Double: | €60-€70 |
| Single: | €35-€40 |
| Dinner | None |
| Open | All year except Christmas |
| Credit Cards | Visa MC Amex |
| Directions | 11/2 miles outside Thomastown on road to Mount Juliet |

Email        belmorehouse@eircom.net
www.lucindaosullivan.com/belmorehouse

# cullintra house

## INISTIOGUE

Inistiogue is a magical beautiful village in south Kilkenny on the River Nore, which has always attracted the artistic bohemian types and was the set of the movie Circle of Friends. Up at the top of the hill is the eerily beautiful burnt out ruins of the Woodstock Estate, which has to be seen. Woodstock was burnt down in 1922 after the house had been occupied by the infamous British Force, the Black and Tans.

## CULLINTRA

Just down the road between Inistiogue and The Rower, Patricia Cantlon has her lovely Cullintra House. Patricia is a one off. Statuesque and beautiful with flowing long golden red tresses, she is artistic and bohemian and, like myself, loves cats of which there are any number to be found around the farm. Legendary stories are told of stay's at Patricia's – late candlelit dinners and late breakfasts – time has no relevance at Cullintra so do not expect the dinner gong to go on the dot of 8 p.m. Patricia might be out picking the wild mushrooms at that stage, while you are socializing with your fellow guests, and dinner will not be until after 9 p.m. After all the hard work, Patricia will appear tantalizingly beautiful in a long evening skirt and present a great value multi course excellent dinner. The finest local ingredients are

used and Patricia describes her food as "Irish-French" and it is all very nicely presented at three tables in the diningroom with a log fire burning and soft candles glowing. It is very sociable and relaxed so that you get into conversation and socialize with new people. Cullintra House is on 230 acres and it is a nature lover's paradise and apart from the animals there is a bird sanctuary, which Patricia guards with her life. There is also a trail to a 4,000-year-old cairn on the land and lots of beautiful walks. Outside there is a large Studio/Conservatory with tea and coffee facilities and a woodburner for guests's use. There is no wine licence at Cullintra so you are welcome to bring your own.

| | |
|---|---|
| Owners | Patricia Cantlon |
| Address | The Rower ,Inistioge Co Kilkenny |
| Tel / Fax | 051 423614 |
| No. Of rooms | 6 |
| Price, Double: | €60 -€80 |
| Single: | |
| Dinner | Yes BYO wine |
| Open | All Year |
| Credit Cards | Visa ,MC |
| Directions | Take R700 from New Ross for 6 miles House up road on right |
| Email | |

www.lucindaosullivan.com/cullintrahouse

# mount juliet conrad

**M**ount Juliet is a magnificent Georgian Mansion overlooking the River Nore on 1500 acres of unspoiled woodland and meandering waters in Thomastown, South Kilkenny, built by the Earl of Carrick. Latterly, Mount Juliet was owned by the late Major Victor McCalmont and his wife Bunty, well known figures on the Irish social scene. Hunting, shootin', fishin', House Parties, were the thing along, with the Dublin Horse Show, Hacking Jackets from Callaghan's of Dame Street, and Louis Wine's Antique Shop. The lives of staff in those days revolved around the big Estate and very often went from generation to generation of minding "the Major" and previous incumbents. Mount Juliet was developed with great foresight and subtlety by Businessman, Tim Mahony, for even though you drive through the Jack Nicklaus designed 18 hole Championship Golf Course, past the self catering Rose Garden Lodges and Hunters Yard complex, the house is far enough away to retain the illusion of being on a private estate and still feels more "Country House" than Hotel. Now part of the Conrad Hotel Group, if your days aren't filled with golf or country pursuits you can chill out and be pampered at the Health Club and Spa. There are two Restaurants, the Lady Helen Diningroom, with really superb food. Albert Roux the famous french chef comes to Mount Juliet

to shoot and he cooked the favourite soufflé of the late Queen Mother for us. The other dining option is Kendals Restaurant in the Hunters Yard which is large and buzzy. The rooms in the main house are gracious and beautiful and the modern rooms in the Hunters yard are super. Breakfast in the Lady Helen Room overlooking the River, rolling acres and romping young cattle, is simply bliss with a tremendous array of fresh, dried and exotic fruits, pastries, French yogurts, cheeses, cold cuts, smoothies, porridge with fresh cream or honey, pancakes with maple syrup, cinnamon sugar and Wexford strawberries. "Would you like to try Tiger's Breakfast"? asked Donal Cahill, the Restaurant Manager. I was still romancing about the classy Colonial days, Indiaaah and all that, forgetting that more recent blow in, Tiger Woods, until I was enlightened. Anyway, Tiger's breakfast is stacked French toast and smoked salmon topped with poached eggs. You might fancy "The Major's breakfast" which delves into the nether regions of liver and kidneys- strong stuff first thing. Mount Juliet is a glorious place, it is not just the house and nice staff, but the lushness of the grounds and winding paths which are a constant reminder of another life – people crave peace and space they will find it all here.

| | |
|---|---|
| Owners | Andrew Phelan (General Manager) |
| Address | Thomastown, Co Kilkenny |
| Tel / Fax | 056 7773000 /056 7773019 |
| No. Of rooms | 58 |
| Price, Double/Twin | From €209 |
| Single: | From €192 |
| Family | From €385 |
| Dinner | Yes – 2 Restaurants |
| Open | All Year |
| Credit Cards | Visa MC Diners Amex |
| Directions | Follow signs from Thomastown |
| Email | info@mountjuliet.ie |

www.lucindaosullivan.com/mountjuliet

# county laois

Laois is a very unassuming and modest county, which does little to blow its own trumpet but does have its share of interesting history. For example, the county's principal town of Portlaoise was originally named Maryborough after Mary Tudor of Britain. It is a thriving business town and site of the Republic's main prison, which has housed many of the political prisoners during the recent "troubles". Ten miles south of Portlaoise is Abbeyleix, named after a Cistercian Abbey founded there in 1183 but the village was vastly altered in the 18th century by the Viscount De Vesci whose descendants resided there until very recently. Stradbally is well known for its Steam Museum and its narrow gauge railway where a 19th century steam locomotive, formerly used in the Guinness Brewery, runs about six times a year. If you are driving beware of your speed when approaching Cullahill on your way south for I have sad memories of being caught in a speed trap there, and me in reverse!

"Modesty is the art of encouraging people to find out for themselves how wonderful you are"

(Anon)

Preston house

When I was a child we used stay near Abbeyleix, as my Uncle was a Curate of the Parish, so I knew the area pretty well. That was in the days when Earl and Countess de Vesci lived in Abbeyleix in the big estate. There is always something about a town that has the remnants of auld decency about it. I had a Siamese cat whose name was Suzuki San and she was entered in the local Agricultural Show – she was a rare sight in a midland town then. Suzi won second prize, which didn't qualify for a ribbon, and I felt so hurt for her – home we went in Uncle's car and out came the blue ribbon and the biggest bestest rosette ever ensued. Abbeyleix has an excellent heritage centre but for heritage of another sort drop into Morrissey's Bar.

## PRESTON HOUSE

Alison and Michael Dowling's Preston House, on the main street in Abbeyleix, is quite rightly admired and lauded by everyone who ever visits there, be it just for lunch or dinner passing through, or staying overnight. The Georgian creeper clad original schoolhouse is delightfully warm and welcoming. Walk through the door and you will be assailed with appetizing aromas from the kitchen, which is always a good omen. There is a tremendous buzz as people pour in at lunchtime for Alison's wonderful food – wholesome, fresh, thoughtful and innovative – just as she is herself a no nonsense person with a tremendous warmth and friendliness. Here you will see the local Bank Manager, Parish Priest or Doctor, unable to resist what is going to be on Alison's menu today, but you definitely need to get in early for a table in this lovely Restaurant straight out of Country Life. Dense pungent smoked haddock chowder is legendary as is the chicken liver pate. Mainers might include salmon with hollandaise or a fine fillet of cod

cooked to perfection and served with a lemon butter sauce accompanied by wholesome fresh vegetables and wonderful potatoes. All you have to do after dinner is toddle upstairs, no driving, and look forward to yet more wonderful food at breakfast. The bedrooms are great, full of atmosphere, with big comfortable beds, T.V. magazines, sofas, and pine floors scattered with rugs. Preston House is a stress free old schoolhouse offering comfort and divine home cooked food from a country loving family.

| Owners | Michael and Alison Dowling |
|---|---|
| Address | Abbeyleix ,Co Laois. |
| Tel / Fax | 0502 31432 /050231432 |
| No. Of rooms | 4 |
| Price, Double: | € 90 |
| Single: | € 50 |
| Dinner | Yes |
| Open | All Year except Christmas |
| Credit Cards | Visa MC |
| Directions | On the Cork side of Abbeyleix town |

Email        prestonhouse@eircom.net
www.lucindaosullivan.com/prestonhouse

# county limerick

imerick City, located at the lowest fording point of the River Shannon, is sports mad whether it be Gaelic football, hurling, horse racing, soccer or particularly rugby football which boasts that well known Limerick invention the "Garryowen":- the high kick forward which allows your team to charge after it and put the fear of God into the poor player who happens to be trying to catch it. It is also famous as the location of Frank McCourt's book *Angela's Ashes*, although some of

its inhabitants find it hard to accept. From the time the Vikings sailed up the Shannon and settled there, the place has had a troubled history but it is probably best remembered for the Williamite Siege in the late 1600's resisted by the Irish, led by Patrick Sarsfield. Probably the best-known tourist attraction in the city is the Hunt Museum, which has a collection to rival Dublin's National Gallery. In the late 1930's and early 1940's, Foynes was the terminus for the transatlantic Flying Boat service, and is home now to a Flying Boat Museum. Kilmallock and its nearby Museum is only four miles from Bruree, whose claim to fame is that it was the childhood home of Eamonn de Valera, former prominent 1916 figure, Taoiseach, and President of Ireland. The gem in the county's crown is the beautiful picturesque village of Adare which has many up market fine antique shops, friendly pubs, excellent Restaurants and art shops but also has a number of beautifully maintained thatched cottages and is regarded as the prettiest village in Ireland.

"The one duty we have to history is to re-write it"
(Oscar Wilde)

# dunraven arms

**E**very November I look forward to an invitation from my horsey
friends to The Hunt Ball in Adare. Whilst a night of tallyho
with the equine fraternity of Limerick has its own special
appeal, the real appeal for His Nibs and myself is to escape to
Irelands prettiest village and stay in The Dunraven Arms, which
never disappoints. This year was no exception and even though it
was a bleak mid winter evening when we descended on Adare the
village looked stunning with its many thatched cottages, up market
restaurants, funky art galleries, and serious Antique Shops. The
Dunraven Arms with its richly painted walls and limestone trim
stands out like a beacon of light and welcome in Adare Built in
1792 it is wonderfully stylish, lavishly furnished with antiques, and
one is always assured of a warm welcome. We arrived early
afternoon in time for a swim in the leisure centre and for me a
facial. Bedrooms are beautiful, spacious with fine bathrooms. Suites

and Junior Suites are superb, with seating areas and dressing rooms. Absolute Bliss. I have had many an encounter with shoddy service delivered by souls that possess what I call "The After the Party Look", not so in Dunraven Arms… There was an abundance of extremely well groomed, well trained and very helpful staff to cater to our every whim. On the morning after, when we trundled down to breakfast, many of us bearing the aforementioned "After The Party Look" there was a feast of freshly squeezed juices of all types, platters of fruit, bowls of Cereals, steaming hot silver pots of tea, and lovely breads but, best of all, hidden under a Silver Dome was the most delicious baked ham which is their Sunday morning specialty. From all of my friends who have stayed at the Dunraven Arms, I have never heard anything but high praise and but I can guarantee you that I would walk barefoot on broken glass back to the Dunraven Arms just for a sliver of that Honey Baked ham. The food is tops, the service is excellent, the location is stunning. Golly Gosh Old Boy an all round Corker.

| | |
|---|---|
| Owners | Louis and Bryan Murphy |
| Address | Adare, Co Limerick |
| Tel / Fax | 061 396633 /061 396541 |
| No. Of rooms | 74 |
| Price, Double: | €152-€190 + 12.5% |
| Single: | €130-€170 + 12.5% |
| Breakfast | €18 + 12.5% |
| Dinner | Yes – 2 Restaurants |
| Open | All Year |
| Credit Cards | Visa MC Diners Amex |
| Directions | On the right as you enter Adare village from N21 from Limerick direction |

Email
reservations@dunravenhotel.com
www.lucindaosullivan.com/dunravenarmshotel

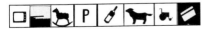

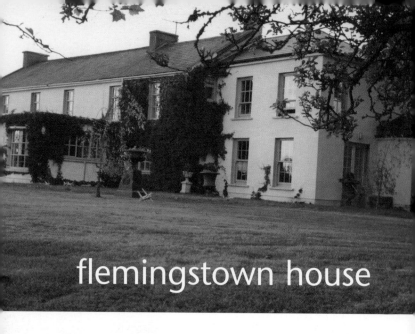

# flemingstown house

Class Reunions, well in fact any event where women gather together, are always fantastic occasions, once each has firmly established that she has the BEST JOB, the BEST HOUSE, the BEST CHILDREN, the BEST CLUB MEMBERSHIPS and, of course, the RICHEST and BEST LOOKING PARTNER – new or otherwise. Having safely dispatched two friends from such a gathering in a sealed plane back to Boston from Shannon I needed a place to thaw out in solitude. I left Limerick and headed south to the medieval town of Kilmallock. Co Limerick is dotted with Castles, some of which are exquisitely restored, but the ones I passed that day were mostly in ruins and being used as scratching poles for the fine fat cattle that grazed happily in the flat lands of the Golden Vale. Imelda Sheedy-King's delightfully restored 18th Century Flemingstown House is really lovely, immaculately furnished in classical timeless style with antique furniture and pretty drapes. The house has been in the family for five generations and enjoys panoramic views of the Ballyhoura Mountains and is ideally situated for golfers or those interested in other field pursuits. Children will love watching the cows being milked. Dinner is available with notice and Imelda is an excellent cook so you can look forward to home cooked food and farm produce, the best of beef, breads, jams, cakes, Farmhouse cheeses and fruits from the garden. Note the beautiful stained glass windows in the conservatory style diningroom. The five large en-suite bedrooms are serene and peaceful overlooking the farm, and

the sweet smell of freshly laundered linen and a little bird singing outside my window soon lulled me to sleep. Next morning I was like new and had a delicious breakfast, which wasn't surprising, as Imelda has won the National Breakfast Award – along with many other awards. Don't forget to do a bit of antiquing in Rathkeale and Adare. Flemingstown House is perfect for exploring Tipperary, Kerry and Limerick and delightful for a weekend away.

| | |
|---|---|
| Owners | Imelda Sheedy -King |
| Address | Kilmallock, Co Limerick |
| Tel / Fax | 063 98093 / 06398546 |
| No. Of rooms | 5 |
| Price, Double: | € 90- €100 |
| Single: | |
| Dinner | Yes – Book |
| Open | Yes |
| Credit Cards | Visa MC |
| Directions | Take R512 to Kilmallock then go on Fermoy Road for 2 miles, house on left |
| Email | info@flemingstown.com |
| | www.lucindaosullivan.com/flemingstownhouse |

# county longford

Bordered by Ireland's greatest river, the Shannon in the west and counties Westmeath and Cavan in the east, Longford is a quiet peaceful midland county with pleasant rolling countryside. It is reckoned that Pallas, 10 miles north of Glasson, is the birthplace of Oliver Goldsmith, author of "She Stoops to Conquer" and "The Vicar of Wakefield".

Longford Town is a large busy rambling place and home of St. Mel's Cathedral – and a pleasant restful spot. For the tourist interested in archaeology a visit to Corlea Trackway Visitor Centre (April – September), nine miles south of Longford is well worthwhile.

Three miles northeast of the Town is Carriglass Manor with its gardens and Costume Museum, open to the public from May to September. Carriglass was built in 1837, by Thomas Lefroy, who was probably the model for Mr. Darcy in "Pride and Prejudice" as, at one stage, he and Jane Austen were romantically involved. The house is still owned by the Lefroy family.

"The very essence of romance is uncertainty. If ever I get married, I'll certainly try to forget the fact."

(Oscar Wilde)

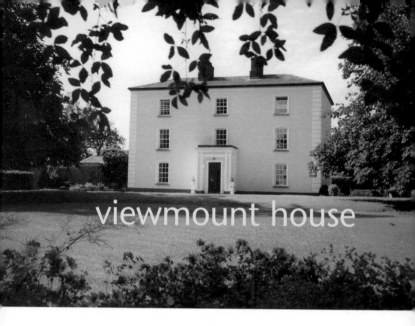

viewmount house

I went with a friend on a skite up to Co. Leitrim a couple of years ago to investigate a French Restaurant called Cuisto Perigord, in the pretty village of Dromahair . It seemed quite extraordinary to find this large purpose built Restaurant in a fairly remote part of Ireland but we enjoyed it thoroughly.

On our way back to Dublin, we spotted Viewmount, an absolutely beautiful house built in 1740 by the Cuffe family. Viewmount was inherited by Thomas Packenham (first Baron of Longford) when he married Elizabeth Cuffe for, "What's your is mine" was the rule of thumb when husbands took a wife in those days. Viewmount has had various distinguished residents and in the late 19th Century was occupied by Harry McCann a famed gardener. James and Beryl Kearney have continued the gardening tradition for the house today sits on four acres of magnificent gardens which are "supervised" by Oisin the friendly Irish Wolfhound. Stroll with Oisin amongst the knot garden, herbaceous borders, Japanese garden, the blue grey garden or white garden, it is sublime. From the splendid red hall with open fire, a fine elegant staircase spirals up to big beautiful bedrooms, very stylishly decorated and furnished with antiques, big beds and rugs. The purple room is divine. From the bedrooms too there are serene views over the garden and the adjoining Longford Golf Club. Breakfast is served in the vaulted diningroom and includes fruits and mueslies, pancakes with maple syrup and pecan nuts, or scrambled eggs with smoked salmon … After that you can visit the exquisite Belvedere House where Robert Rochfort imprisoned his wife, Mary

Molesworth, for 31 years and also see Ireland's largest man made folly – The Jealous Wall. Nearby too is the beautiful Strokestown House with its famine museum. There is a lot of fishing about on Lough Gowna, Lough Ree and the River Shannon. Viewmount is a delightful house to visit for a break or ideal for stopping over on the way to Donegal or the far West.

| Owners | James and Beryl Kearney |
|---|---|
| Address | Dublin Road, Longford |
| Tel / Fax | 043 41919 /043 42906 |
| No. Of rooms | 6 |
| Price, Double/Twin/Suite | € 90-€120 |
| Single: | None |
| Family | €45pps + (children half price) |
| Dinner | No |
| Open | All Year |
| Credit Cards | Visa MC Amex |
| Directions | On Dublin road out of Longford |
| Email | info@viewmounthouse.com |

www.lucindaosullivan.com/viewmounthouse

"No great artist ever sees things as they really are.
If he did, he would cease to be an artist."
(Oscar Wilde)

# county mayo

Mayo is a beautiful county with a landscape of high cliffs, lonely mountains and fuchsia hedges and is renowned as the home of Grace O'Malley, the notorious female pirate, rustler, and rebel whose story is a book in itself. Grace's stronghold was at Clew Bay, which is close to the Pilgrim Mountain of Croagh Patrick, the highest mountain in the area. It is from this spot that Ireland's patron Saint is said to have rid the country of snakes. To the left is the Mweelrea Mountain as seen from Delphi Mountain Resort and Spa. Off to the east, situated snugly between Lough Conn and Lough Cullin is Pontoon, an ideal base for exploring the shores of the lakes or for casting a fishing line. Further east is Knock, well known for its shrine and apparition but now also known for the International Airport at Charlestown nearby. In the south is Cong, site of the ruined 12th Century Cong Abbey, and where the mountains of Connemara give way to the fertile farmland of east Mayo. Probably the best-known centre in Mayo is the Georgian town of Westport, a popular playground for travelers who wish to get away from the wild western countryside. During the summer the town is very popular with visitors from all over Europe and the United States who return annually to enjoy once again its many charms and also to take in its Art Festival.

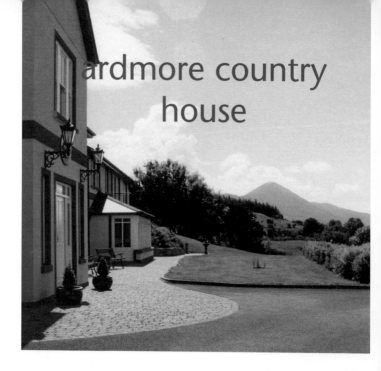

# ardmore country house

## WESTPORT

Having traveled the length and breath of Ireland, I know only too well that wherever you stay can literally make or break your visit and leave an indelible memory. Unfortunately, my first visit to Westport was destroyed by rude receptionists, a stained bed, a dirty room, and bad food and I won't even go into the after effects of that visit but it took six months to recover. Now, if we had only known of Ardmore Country House Hotel and this is where I can short circuit disastrous trips for you. <ep>

## ARDMORE HOUSE HOTEL

Westport is a busy tourist orientated Town, very pretty, lying on the water, within the shadows of a Great House - the famous 18th C. Westport House belonging to the Altamont family. Located just 3 kms from the centre of the town is Pat and Noreen Hoban's Ardmore Country House, stunningly located overlooking Clew Bay, in the shadow of Croagh Patrick, with breathtaking sunsets, and within walking distance of the gates of Westport House. Ardmore's 13 very large and spacious bedrooms are dramatically and stylishly furnished with luxurious fabrics, wonderful colours and have all the little extras, one expects nowadays in top hotels, including a turndown service, power showers and good toiletries. Bedroom prices vary depending on whether they are to the front

of the house with spectacular sea views, or enjoy a rural outlook to the rear. Open fires and a tinkling grand piano are what you can expect to enjoy at Ardmore after a delicious dinner in the Restaurant. Pat Hoban is the Chef/Patron and Ardmore specializes in spanking fresh seafood from Clew Bay, including scallops and lobster, when available. Carnivores are not ignored because prime Irish beef, lamb and wild foul also feature widely. Organic vegetables and herbs from local producers are the order of the day along with an excellent selection of Irish farmhouse cheeses. There is also an extensive wine list with affordable, as well as fine wines, from all the de rigueur Chateaux, for the discerning connoisseur. Ardmore is a grown up place and unsuitable for children under 12. Pat and Noreen are warm and friendly hosts who will only want to ensure that you enjoy your stay with them and see to your every comfort.

| | |
|---|---|
| Owners | Pat Hoban |
| Address | Westport, Co Mayo, Ireland |
| Tel / Fax | 098 25994 / 098 27795 |
| No. Of rooms | 13 |
| Price, Double: | €150-€ 240 |
| Single: | € 100-€145 |
| Dinner | Restaurant on Premises |
| Open | March-December |
| Credit Cards | Visa, MC, Amex |
| Directions | Leave Westport on R335 Louisburg /Coast road for 3Km , watch for sign, |
| Email | ardmorehotel@eircom.net |

www.lucindaosullivan.com/ardmorehousehotel

# pontoon bridge hotel

We all love a short break away from the family with the girls, likewise the boys like to head off too and there is no doubt but you return to the fray refreshed and revitalized after a few days escapism.

### PONTOON BRIDGE HOTEL

Pontoon Bridge Hotel is a mecca for people who love the water and for anglers in their droves. It has featured on the BBC Holiday programme and on ITV's Wish You Were Here. The location is absolutely stunning, set on a narrow peninsula right between Lough Conn and Lough Cullin, and with a gallery of mountain ranges, Nephin and Ox, as a backdrop. The Pontoon Bridge Hotel was built as a Hotel at the end of the 19th Century – just think about it – it's a long time ago. It was bought in 1964 by Brendan and Ann Geary who have made it what it is today. Their children grew up in the family business, gaining their experience on the ground, and now, in 2004, the next generation is in charge bursting with drive and development plans. Daughter Breeta Geary is the General Manager, whilst her sister, Mary, is the Executive Chef and, with other family members involved all over the place, there is a tremendous personal interest in the Hotel, and you, all the time. Apart from the fishing and other outdoor activities, the Pontoon Bridge Hotel run various courses which make great occasions for short breaks away with the girls, or the

boys. They have a Cookery School in which Mary and her team run 2 day courses, primarily informative, but also great fun. There are Landscape Painting Courses with Pat Goff, plus the Pontoon Bridge Hotel School of Fly-fishing, so you can paint and he can learn to fish and whatever you do there will be plenty to talk about in the evenings in the Bar after a fine dinner prepared by Mary Geary and her team. 17 more rooms and extra disabled facilities will be on stream this year and a new Spa and Leisure facilities are planned for 2005.

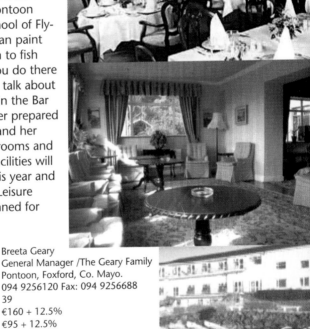

| | |
|---|---|
| Owners | Breeta Geary General Manager /The Geary Family |
| Address | Pontoon, Foxford, Co. Mayo. |
| Tel / Fax | 094 9256120 Fax: 094 9256688 |
| No. Of rooms | 39 |
| Price, Double/Twin | €160 + 12.5% |
| Single: | €95 + 12.5% |
| Dinner | €38-€45 + 10% or Bar Menu |
| Open | All Year save 23rd – 26th December |
| Credit Cards | Visa. MC. Amex. |
| Directions | |
| Email | relax@pontoonbridge.com www.lucindaosullivan.com/pontoonbridgehotel |

rosturk woods

I never think of Mulranny but I remember as a child my father's fishing trip away with his friend Harold. Proudly presenting his catch for cooking at breakfast, he received it back on the plate stinking to high heaven, as the young chef on duty, in what was then the Mulranny Hotel, didn't know it should be cleaned out first! You won't have that problem because you can stay in either of Louisa and Alan Stoney's two beautiful self-catering houses at Rosturk Woods. One has 3 bedrooms; the other 4, so bring Granny. The houses are very comfortably furnished with a mixture of antiques, pine and modern furniture, good heating systems, open fires, and well-equipped kitchens. The houses too are made up when you arrive, so no drudgery, and there is no charge for bedlinen or towels. Mulranny is a magnificent place, close to Achill Island, with amazing rhododendrons – just stunningly beautiful. Both houses have views facing south to Clew Bay with private access to the tidal beach in front – just fantastic. Great in summer or winter with the spacious rooms filled with the light off the sea. Lots of wildlife, including otters and other creatures. Fascinating for adults or kids alike. Rosturk Woods, on five acres, is heaven for those either wanting peace and quiet or for families with kids who would enjoy the space and exercise. Lots of boating potential as well as swimming and windsurfing. There are wheelchair facilities in the 4 bedroomed house and there is a tennis court and Games room on site. Pets are welcome so you can even bring Fido. There

are Restaurants in Westport,
Newport and one at Mulranny
(not of uncleaned fish fame), if
you want to eat out occasionally.
Louisa and Alan are warm
welcoming hosts – you will like
them.

| | |
|---|---|
| Owners | Alan and Louisa Stoney |
| Address | Rosturk, Mulranny, Westport, Co. Mayo. |
| Tel / Fax | 098 36264 /09836264 |
| Self Catering | Low Season €650/€750 3 bedroomed House Shoulder Season €750/ €900 4 bedroomed House High Season €975/€1200 (High Season incs Easter/Christmas/New Year) |
| Dinner | No |
| Open | All Year |
| Credit Cards | No |
| Directions | From Newport take N59 Mulranny/Achill Road for 7 miles. Look for sign on left. |
| Email | stoney@iol.ie www.lucindaosullivan.com/rosturkwoods |

# county monaghan

Probably one of County Monaghan's most famous sons was Poet, Patrick Kavanagh, a magical wordsmith with a mammoth thirst. Born in Inniskeen, his work often evokes the poor quality of peasant life in the County in former times. Monaghan Town is now a busy commercial centre and was the residence of Charles Gavin Duffy in the 19th Century. He was instrumental in founding both the Young Ireland Movement and the Irish Tenants League and was co-founder with Thomas Davis of The Nation, a politically inspired Newspaper. He emigrated to Australia in 1856 and became Speaker of the Australian Assembly in 1877. There are two main routes out of Monaghan Town – west to the town of Clones and its well known Gaelic Football Ground, or south to Carrickmacross which is famous for its beautiful handmade lace. Like very other Irish County there is no shortage of entertainment and bars providing both traditional ballads and nowadays Café Bars.

"Every St. Patrick's Day, every Irishman goest out to find another Irishman to make a speech to".

(Shane Leslie).

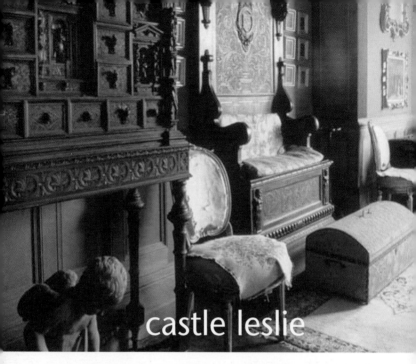

# castle leslie

Castle Leslie is just fabulously fabulously fabulous, which no doubt is why Sir Paul McCartney chose to wed Heather Mills here. Sammy Leslie has done much to preserve her wonderful ancestral pile and heritage, which can't be easy in this day and age, for we all know how much it costs to get a plumber and a gardener for an ordinary house. Wait until you see Castle Leslie's loos, their three lakes and rolling acres abounding with ancient oaks, and realize what they are up against. From the oak paneled hall to the beautiful drawingroom, it is a wonderful experience and nothing can quite prepare you for it. Dinner in the diningroom, which has not seen change in the last 100 years, on tables that have been used by the Leslie family for generations, is glorious. The 14 bedrooms are decorated in differing styles – lavish and magnificent. The rich Red Room is regal, lush and imperial. The Mauve Room is also known as the Royal Suite as Queen Margaret of Sweden and a few other noble heads have rested there over the years. Not quite so noble, if also recently titled, Sir Mick of the Jaggers slept there too in his Marianne Faithful days, when the not so faithful Sir Mick was chased around the pond by screaming wayward girls from a reform school on a picnic. The Chinese Room used to have a secret passage – very handy for illicit assignations – however it was closed when the last romantic to use it fell through a ceiling. You might fancy Papa Jack's, the Governess' Suite or any other of the fantasy rooms for a

romp in the hay … From time to time they have special gourmet weekends with communal tables. They are fun, the Leslies, not eccentric as they are often described but interesting, arty and theatrical and they can trace their ancestry back to Attila the Hun – can you? The first Leslie came to Ireland from Scotland, and he was Hungarian, but their family history is the stuff of novels, they seem to be related to everyone from Jenny Jerome, the American heiress, who was Winston Churchill's mother – see his romper suit on display - to the Duke of Wellington.. You will have gathered that there is nothing stuffy about Castle Leslie and despite all the so called eccentricities be assured that where Sammy Leslie is concerned she runs Her Castle with total professionalism and you will be wonderfully looked after - and you will have experienced something really special.

| | | | | |
|---|---|---|---|---|
| P | | | | |

| | |
|---|---|
| Owners | Sammy Leslie |
| Address | Glaslough , Co Monaghan. |
| Tel / Fax | 047 88109 / 047 88256 |
| No. Of rooms | 14 |
| Price, Double: | €250-€350 |
| Single: | |
| Dinner | Yes |
| Open | All year |
| Credit Cards | All major cards |
| Directions | Signed posted on Monaghan –Armagh road near Glaslough |
| Email | info@castleleslie.com |

www.lucindaosullivan.com/castleleslie

# county roscommon

Sitting to write about County Roscommon brings back happy memories of many weeks spent boating on the River Shannon, which borders the county to the east. We would rent a cruiser in Jamestown and sail downriver under the bridge at Roosky past Tarmanbarry into beautiful Lough Ree and on down through Athlone et al. We did occasionally stop for a little drop of nourishment in some of the friendly pubs on the way. Roscommon town a pleasant place for a visit has the quaint story about its County Jail, now housing a collection of shops and restaurants. Apparently it was the scene of all the hangings in the county and used to have a woman executioner by the name of Lady Betty. She had her own sentence for murder revoked provided she did the job unremunerated. Strokestown is a well-planned town with an exceptionally wide main street, the idea of some former bigwig who wanted to boast the widest street in Europe. Strokestown Park House, designed by Richard Cassels, with its beautiful gardens and Famine Museum is well worth a visit. Heading west from Strokestown through Tulsk, the home of the legendary Queen Medb, who caused her share of trouble, you come upon Frenchpark, which gave the country its first President, Douglas Hyde, who was also one of the founders of the Gaelic League. Go south a little to Castlerea where it is worth stopping to visit Clonalis, which is the ancestral home of the O'Conor Clan, Kings of Connaught. Clonalis House has a number of interesting paintings charting the family's colourful history at home and abroad. To the north of the county is the town of Boyle on the banks of a river of the same name, an area that has become attractive to many artists, musicians and crafts people and warrants a visit to the Cistercian Boyle Abbey consecrated in 1220.

"Between two evils, I always pick the one I never tried before."
(Mae West)

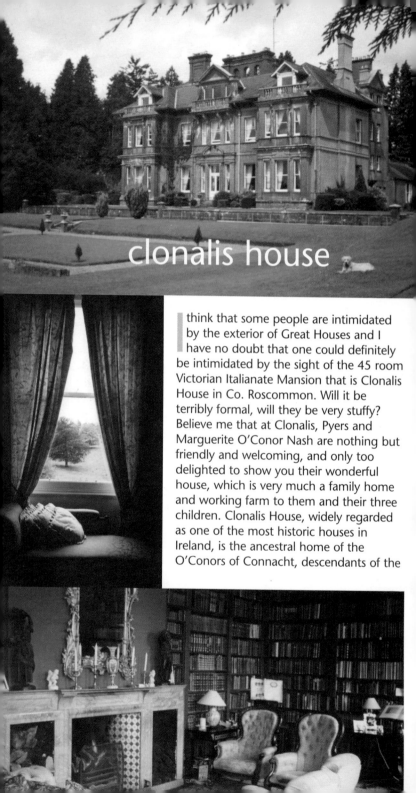

# clonalis house

I think that some people are intimidated by the exterior of Great Houses and I have no doubt that one could definitely be intimidated by the sight of the 45 room Victorian Italianate Mansion that is Clonalis House in Co. Roscommon. Will it be terribly formal, will they be very stuffy? Believe me that at Clonalis, Pyers and Marguerite O'Conor Nash are nothing but friendly and welcoming, and only too delighted to show you their wonderful house, which is very much a family home and working farm to them and their three children. Clonalis House, widely regarded as one of the most historic houses in Ireland, is the ancestral home of the O'Conors of Connacht, descendants of the

last High Kings of Ireland and traditional Kings of Connacht, and the land has been in the O'Conor family for 1500 years. The house was built in 1878 and sits on an estate of 750 acres nestling in a crescent of cypress and redwood trees. There is much to see at Clonalis including a copy of the last Brehon Law Judgment (handed down about 1580) and The O'Conor Coronation Stone. Pyers and Marguerite O'Conor Nash have restored the old walled garden and, for anglers, there are two brown trout rivers on which to cast a line. Bedrooms are simply beautiful, with four-posters, half testers, gilt frame mirrors, fabulous antiques and massive bathrooms, and have spectacular views out over the formal gardens. Marguerite is a wonderful cook and providing fresh Country House food from Tuesday to Saturday, which is served in the fabulous diningroom hung with portraits of the ancestors. Have a pre-dinner drink in the library. Here you can live out your dream of staying in a mansion and you can also make new friends around the communal table but, if you really want "to be alone" that can be arranged too with a separate table. Not suitable for children under 12. A visit to Clonalis will really be something to tell your friends about … I wonder how they manage 45 rooms … the mind boggles

| | |
|---|---|
| Owners | Pyers and Marguerite O Conor Nash |
| Address | Castlerea , Co Roscommon |
| Tel / Fax | 094 9620014 /094 9620014 |
| No. Of rooms | 4 |
| Price, Double: | €132-€156 10% Reduction on stays of over 3 nights |
| Single: | |
| Dinner | Tuesday-Saturday 24 hours notice required |
| Open | Mid April – September 30th |
| Credit Cards | Visa MC |
| Directions | N61 Athlone – Roscommon. Bypass to N60 to Castlerea |
| Email | clonalis@iol.ie |
| | www.lucindaosullivan.com/clonalis |

# county tipperary

Tipperary is the largest of Ireland's inland counties. Situated in the rich fertile lands of the Golden Vale it is also a very wealthy county. Without a doubt, the most outstanding of its many attractions is the Rock of Cashel, rising sharply to over 200 feet and topped by mediaeval walls and buildings. Not far from Cashel is the peaceful town of Cahir on the River Suir with its wonderful Castle dating back to the 13th and the 15th centuries, an Anglo Norman stronghold of the Butlers, the Earls of Ormond. North of Cashel the River Suir passes through the towns of Thurles, not far from Holy Cross Abbey, and is the birthplace of the G.A.A., the ruling body for our National Games. Templemore is like Westpoint on flat feet, being the training headquarters of the Irish Police Force, the Garda Siochana. The area around Nenagh and Lough Derg – Terryglass, Coolbaun, Puckaun -is very popular now with many people having holiday homes near the Lake. Nenagh also boasts a colossal round Castle Keep with walls 20 feet thick and a height of 100 feet topped with 19th century castellations. Clonmel is probably Tipperary's prettiest centre. It was the principal base for Bianconi, the most successful coach company in the 1800's in this country. Clonmel also boasts the 19th century St. Mary's Roman Catholic Church, the 19th century West Gate and the Greek Revival style Wesleyan Church and more. The county has many peaceful and pleasant villages to appeal to visitors such as Bansha, not far from Cahir and backed by the Glen of Aherlow and the Galtee Mountains, or Ballyporeen whose claim to fame is that U.S. President Ronald Regan's grandfather hailed from there.

"An actor's a guy who, if you ain't talking about him, ain't listening"

(Marlon Brando)

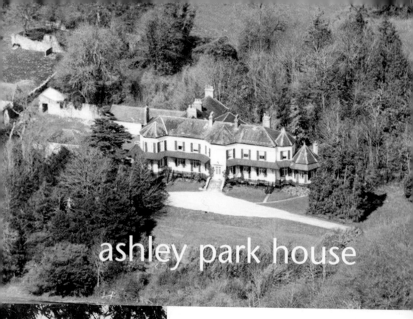

# ashley park house

The first time I saw Ashley Park House I took a deep intake of breath and thought I had entered the film set of Gone With the Wind or Raintree County. It is a most dramatic and unusual house for this part of the world and would do Savannah proud. An 18th Century house, a white vision with elaborate green painted verandahs, overlooking the sultry Lake Ourne with hanging weeping trees. Ashley Park is on 76 acres of beechwood and formal gardens with strolling peacocks, ancient walled gardens, and is quite spellbinding. Friend Carmel and I had whirled up in my little blue MGF open topped car. Sean Mounsey, the family patriarch complete with cap, who is one of the greatest characters you are ever likely to meet said, "I want you to be happy here Ma'am". I felt like Princess Margaret. Sean took us up to the "Bishop's room" where he had put up a small temporary bed beside the half tester as the house was full and looking puzzled said half to himself, "I wasn't expecting two such fine strapping women as yourselves – now if one of you were smaller". Tears streamed down our faces we laughed so much,

and as Carmel collapsed over the dressing table in a heap, Sean Mounsey beat a hasty retreat …

Ashley Park House has some of the finest rooms you will ever come across and you can live out all of your Scarlett O'Hara fantasies in this house. The front bedrooms at either end of the house are vast, splendid and romantic. The house is magnificently furnished, with impeccable taste, by Sean's daughter Margaret. Relax in the magnificent drawingroom with a drink in front of the fire before or after dinner, or chill out in the beautiful octagonal Chinese Reading Room off it. Explore the old walled garden which they are restoring. Dine in the magnificent diningroom. Go to Ashley Park quickly you might not find Rhett Butler but you will find Sean Mounsey and his beautiful daughter Margaret and they are much more interesting altogether. Children are welcome. It is incredible value and an equally incredible experience.

| | |
|---|---|
| Owners | PJ and Margaret Mounsey |
| Address | Ashley Park ,Nenagh ,Co Tipperary,Ireland |
| Tel / Fax | 067 38223  /  067 38013 |
| No. Of rooms | 5 |
| Price, Double:<br>Single: | €90-€110 |

| | |
|---|---|
| Dinner | €35-€40  Book by 2PM |
| Open | All Year |
| Credit Cards | Visa. MC. Diners. AMEX |
| Directions | From Nenagh turn right on N52  for 3 miles Ashley Park is the large white house on the opposite side of Lake |
| Email | margaret@ashleypark.com<br>www.lucindaosullivan.com/ashleyparkhouse |

baileys of cashel

I f walls could speak then Bailey's Townhouse would keep a listener enthralled for hours. This very fine house was built in 1703 by the Wesley Family, so is just over 300 years old and has a great history. Dermot and Phil Delaney, who have an excellent pedigree in hospitality, bought the house not so long ago and have totally revamped and upgraded it. Phil's impeccable taste is evident from the moment you set foot on the black and white tiled floor of the Hall with its lovely Farrow & Ball colors. The bedrooms are beautifully furnished and all have data terminals so no matter how far from home you are, you will always be able to stay in contact. Being so centrally located you can just leave the car and walk around returning for a casual lunch or to the drawing room to relax. Breakfast is served in the green dining room looking out on the wealthy streets of Cashel. The Cellar Restaurant downstairs complete with open fire and a well stocked bar has a very wide menu serving casual food at lunchtime and lots on offer too for dinner. Phil is a natural cook and a generous one to boot. She is the type of Chef who bakes two types of bread for Sunday Lunch crusty white soda bread and a dark brown bread. Service is supervised by their vivacious daughter who is studying Hotel Management. Bailey's is a superb place to stay when visiting Ireland's most famous monument, the famous Rock of Cashel. It is also a great spot for a short break – there are lots of golf clubs and pubs and places to see such as the Cashel folk village, Cahir Castle, the picture postcard Swiss Cottage at Cahir and much much more. Oh if you want a bit of ceoil and rince there are sesiuns in the Bru Boru Heritage Centre from June to September.

| | |
|---|---|
| Owners | Phil Delaney |
| Address | Main Street, Cashel, Co Tipperary. |
| Tel / Fax | 062 61937  /062 63957 |
| No. Of rooms | 9 |
| Price, Double: | €80 |
| Single: | €50-€55 |
| Dinner | Restaurant |
| Open | All Year |
| Credit Cards | Visa MC AMEX |
| Directions | |
| Email | |

info@baileys-ireland.com
www.lucindaosullivan.com/baileysguesthouse

# bansha castle

got a tall order from an English PR agency representing the Boss of a large Legal Firm. The Boss was suffering Hip Hotel Fatigue so looking for something different. He wanted to rent a big Country House where he could entertain his best customers for a week. If it was that simple I would, as they say in Tipperary, be away in a hack, but no, he wanted more and a lot more. He wanted a house where he could self cater and indulge his passion for cooking some nights and have dinner provided other nights. Still simple, you may say, but he also wanted a place where he and his friends could hunt, shoot and fish and be within walking distance of the local pub  Well you will be delighted to know that I found the perfect retreat at the 18th century  Bansha Castle. As I travelled the road from Cashel to Bansha it reminded me a little of Beverly Hills without the traffic for it definitely had the mansions, secure stud farms and prime beef units. This is 4-wheel drive territory so I knew when I arrived at Bansha Castle that I had backed a winner for Mr Lawyer. Teresa and John Russell are welcoming hosts and there is a great casual feel to the whole place so you know where one can just throw your riding jacket on the hall stand, and leave your riding boots at the bottom of the stairs, without fear of reprimand. Teresa will organize the huntin' , shootin', fishin' and she can also organize a beautician to come if you want to pamper yourself. The Drawing room is a large room with a full size pool table just off. Perfect for someone with a wasted childhood in Pool Halls or for a visiting member of the

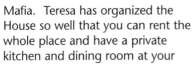

Mafia. Teresa has organized the House so well that you can rent the whole place and have a private kitchen and dining room at your disposal or she will cook Breakfast and Dinner for you at times to suit you If the house is not let then you will have the opportunity to stay on a bed and breakfast basis and also be able to enjoy a dinner at one of her beautifully laid tables in the large Dining Room. This arrangement also suits people celebrating special occasions even divorces and you can bring your own booze.

| Owners | John and Teresa Russell |
| Address | Bansha, Co.Tipperary. Ireland |
| Tel / Fax | 062 54187 /062 54294 |
| No. Of rooms | 6 |
| Price, Double: | €70-€90 |
| Single: | |
| | The Castle is available for self catering It sleeps 12 –17 Price on application |
| Dinner | Yes must be pre booked |
| Open | All Year |
| Credit Cards | None |
| Directions | Located just outside village of Bansha |
| Email | johnrus@iol.ie |

www.lucindaosullivan.com/banshacastle

## Inch House

Eamonn de Valera was President when I was a child. A very old man at that stage, he was almost blind and was an austere and forbidding figure with a black hat sitting up in the back of the old state car. To me he was a terrifying sight and I didn't like him at all. Well, whatever I thought about the man, he got his own back because when I got married I was in a fairly pressured job and when we moved into our new house the timing of the move, arranged three months in advance, was down to seconds. The carpet layers were coming first along with the plumbers. De Valera upped and died and the Nation went into mourning. His funeral was on the day of the move, the carpet layers went out in sympathy, whilst the furniture removers from the old house didn't, hence the furniture arrived first and the carpet layers arrived after dark much the worse for the wear...

### INCH HOUSE

John and Nora Egan's Inch House in Thurles sits proud in the middle of lush farmland with a drive up to the stately front door. The first thing you notice about Inch, is the meticulous care given to the pot plants outside the door – perfectly cared for but the second thing I noticed was the portrait of Dev over my bedroom door!  Get John Egan talking about politics and you could have the fun of your life – he is gregarious and brilliant all in one.  Nora laughs quietly in the background at the good of it all while she overseas this meticulous well cared for house.  Have a drink in the beautiful William Morris papered blue, white and gilt, drawingroom and listen to the local stories.  The Restaurant attracts people from all over the place for the ample well prepared

food served by wonderful ladies who will look after you like a mother.  The House was the former home of the Ryan family for hundreds of years – a great Tipperary name – and in fact shortly after I wrote about Inch House I had an email from the Ryans in New Zealand where they have now made their home.  Have a look at the stained glass Ryan coat of arms on the staircase the family motto was "Death Before Dishonour".  The bedrooms are beautiful, peaceful and comfortable, and you will recline on the finest linen in a Prince Albert bed before coming down to a lavish breakfast in the magnificent diningroom again.  It is a beautiful house on wonderful grounds and I can't wait to go back again.

| Owners | John and Nora Egan |
|---|---|
| Address | Thurles ,Co Tipperary |
| Tel / Fax | 0504 51348/51261  /050451754 |
| No. Of rooms | 5 |
| Price,  Double: | €105 |
| Single: | €60 |
| Dinner | Yes |
| Open | All Year |
| Credit Cards | Visa MC Laser |
| Directions | From Thurles take Nenagh  road for 6 Kms past The Ragg. House is on the left |
| Email | inchhse@iol.ie |

www.lucindaosullivan.com/inchhouse

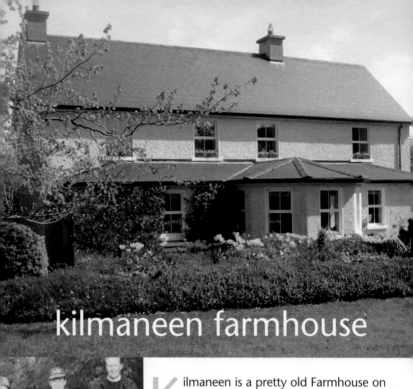

# kilmaneen farmhouse

Kilmaneen is a pretty old Farmhouse on lovely gardens set smack in the middle of three beautiful mountain ranges – the Comeraghs, the Knockmealdowns and the Galtees. Walk with Kevin, a qualified mountain skills leader, who will be happy to share his local knowledge with you. Not only are you lucky enough at Kilmaneen to have a mountain skills leader in residence but both the Rivers Suir and Tar flow through their farmland so whether you are an accomplished angler, or just beginning, you can try your hand at casting a line. In fact you can catch your own dinner or have a trout grilled for breakfast – that will make you a star in the diningroom in the morning. There is an idea that Farmers are not interested in gardening but Kevin disproves this theory rapidly for the garden at Kilmaneen contains many unusual rare plants and trees. In fact, says Bernadette, the whole farm is an on-going gardening project although farmed on a commercial basis. With dairy cows and beef cattle as the main enterprises the rural development is protected and cared for. The four immaculate bedrooms are very pretty, some with toile de jouy wallpaper, all nicely draped and furnished with antiques, but with modern comforts also provided. Bernadette cooks a no choice three

course evening meal, main course, dessert/cheese, tea or coffee, which you must book by that morning. Vegetarian cooking is of special interest to the O'Donnells, but not exclusively so, for they love to serve their own farm reared beef and other farm and home produce. Cashel Blue, roast vegetables and polenta tart with saffron potatoes followed by Eve's Pudding or Crème Brulee with baked plums and vanilla cream would be a typical vegetarian dish. There is no wine licence at Kilmaneen but you are very welcome to bring your own favourite vintage for dinner or to sit out and relax beforehand in the peace of Kevin's lovely garden. It is a non-smoking house and children are welcome. They are delightful people and it is a lovely hidden spot for a breakaway.

| | |
|---|---|
| Owners | Kevin and Bernadette O Donnell |
| Address | New Castle,Clonmel,Co Tipperary. |
| Tel / Fax | 052 36231 /052 36231 |
| No. Of rooms | 4 |
| Price, Double: | €75-€80 |
| Single: | €45 |
| Dinner | Yes BYO Wine |
| Open | March 1st – December 1st off season by arrangement |
| Credit Cards | Visa MC |
| Directions | In Ardfinnan watch for sign at Hill Bar |
| Email | kilmaneen@eircom.net |
| | www.lucindaosullivan.com/kilmaneenfarmhouse |

# county waterford

A walled city of Viking origin, Waterford is the oldest city in Ireland and even today it retains much of its medieval character. It is the home of Waterford Crystal, the world-famous handcrafted, cut glass product. The parameters of the 10th century settlement can be clearly identified in The Viking Triangle. Reginald's Tower is the most historic urban medieval monument in Ireland while the elegant Chamber of Commerce building, the City Hall and the Bishop's Palace are prime examples of beautiful 18th century architecture. Waterford has a long theatrical and musical tradition, which centres on the historic Theatre Royal, which hosts the Waterford International Festival of Light Opera each year. East of the city is the pretty village of Passage East with its ferry service to Ballyhack in Co. Wexford. Stay on the coast road south to the long sandy beach, flanked by woodland, at Woodstown ideal for a quiet stroll or gentle dip in the sea. Go further south to the popular holiday village of Dunmore East which is largely undiscovered by tourists, or go west to the honky tonk family holiday town of Tramore. Further west is the busy commercial town of Dungarvan but swing inland to the beautiful hidden stretch of the River Blackwater around Cappoquin within three miles of Lismore and its ecclesiastical past and most dramatic castle in the country, Lismore Castle, owned by the Duchess of Devonshire. It is a fabulous area and also largely undiscovered by tourists. If you want to learn a few words of the native tongue drive back south to the Irish speaking area of Ring where the language thrives as do other traditions such as music and set dancing.

"Never drink black coffee at lunch, it will keep you awake all afternoon"

(Jilly Cooper attrib)

# foxmount country house

Our French visitors, Michele and Zandra, had expressed a definite interest in visiting the Waterford Glass factory so the decision was taken to drive down and overnight in Waterford. We drove down through Wicklow, the Garden of Ireland, and Wexford and duly did the tour of the Waterford Glass factory. Living in Paris the idea of an Irish Farm appealed and I had one up my sleeve. They took a sharp intake of breath when the ivy clad Foxmount House came into view. "Oh, this is beautiful" they exclaimed of its impeccably kept lawns, glorious flower beds and gravel paths that looked like they had been fine combed. Inside too they were delighted with a blazing fire in the drawingroom as they admired the family silver, antiques and general good taste of Margaret and David Kent who with their son and daughter run this lovely house and dairy farm to perfection. Michele and Zandra were anxious to explore the farm so David took them under his wing and showed them around. Some time later I looked out my lovely bedroom window and was surprised to see the pair of them beating a ball back and forth out on the tennis court, but what struck me most when I gazed out that window was being able to see into Margaret Kent's kitchen where perched on the window sill was a bowl of perfectly arranged soft and dewy pink roses. For me that said it all, Foxmount house is perfection from the sign on the main road right through to the hidden sections of the kitchen. Margaret is a perfectionist and breakfast was just beautifully presented with little bowls of floating flowers and pretty leaves. Dinner is available on Friday and Saturday nights – book in advance – think delicious home produced lamb

with mustard and rosemary sauce and maybe Bailey's Cream Vacherin and strawberries from their garden to follow. You are welcome to bring your own wine. Foxmount, is close to everywhere, Waterford City, the Passage East Ferry, and Dunmore East so is an excellent base to work out east and west from or have a break.

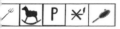

| | |
|---|---|
| Owners | David and Margaret Kent |
| Address | Passage East Road, Waterford |
| Tel / Fax | 051 874308  /051 854906 |
| No. Of rooms | 5 |
| Price, Double: | €110 |
| Single: | |
| Dinner | Yes  Friday and Saturday only |
| Open | Mid March- 1st November |
| Credit Cards | No |
| Directions | Take Dunmore East road from Waterford City, then take Passage East road for 1mile Sign on right |
| Email | info@foxmountcountryhouse.com |
| | www.lucindaosullivan.com/foxmountcountryhouse |

# Gaultier Lodge

It was to Woodstown, a secluded area outside Waterford, that Jackie Kennedy brought her children, John and Caroline, for an away from it all Irish holiday after President Kennedy was assassinated. One can just visualize the children, as they were, playing in the sand and enjoying pony rides, far away from the real world. Woodstown is still an escape, which still seems far away from the real world.

### GAULTIER LODGE

Now don't think for one minute that Jean Paul Gaultier has diversified his mighty clothing empire into the B. & B. business in Waterford! The Gaultier name applies to the Barony of Gaultier, which is all around this area. Sheila Bagliani's Gaultier Lodge is a dream of a house to come upon – a real find. Here is an 18th century Hunting Lodge, designed by John Roberts, backing right onto the most wonderful sandy beach overlooking the widest part of the tidal estuary between County Waterford and County Wexford. Slip on a beach robe and stroll out onto what seems like your own private beach, rush the bracing waves, or just walk and walk and maybe meet no one. Really good for the soul. Bring Fido – and the husband as well if you want – he is allowed outdoors, and even indoors for a small charge, the dog that is. The house is

built on a bank of rock and drops down at the back with the diningroom and kitchen on the lower level. The bedrooms are very spacious and beautifully furnished with views overlooking the beach and bay. Gaultier is a beautiful gracious base for visiting Dunmore East, Tramore, Dungarvan or West Waterford, or indeed even Wexford in the opposite direction because of a little ferry which runs back and forth between Passage East and Ballyhack, linking the two counties in five minutes. There are any number of Golf Courses nearby Waterford, Tramore, Waterford Castle, … and local Hunting is available during the Season. Children over 8 are welcome. Sheila lives in the magnificent Castleffrench in Roscommon and so Gaultier is managed by John and Jill Thomas who will look after you admirably.

| | |
|---|---|
| Owners | Sheila Bagliani |
| Address | Woodstown, Co. Waterford. |
| Tel / Fax | 051 382549 |
| No. Of rooms | 4 |
| Price, Double: | €140 |
| Twin | €130 |
| Single: | €95 |
| Dinner | No |
| Open | May to October other times by arrangement |
| Credit Cards | Visa MC |
| Directions | Take R684 Dunmore East Road from Waterford for 6 miles, then left at sign for Woodstown. Go through village towards beach, right at T junction. Lodge 0.25 miles on left. Behind high wall. At beach. |

Email    castleffrench@eircom.net
www.lucindaosullivan.com/gaultierlodge

# glasha farmhouse

**Y**ou know that great Irish welcome that we all boast about and very often don't find – well you can be sure of it at Olive and Paddy O'Gorman's lovely Glasha Farmhouse set in the beautiful Nire Valley. It is a large white house impeccably maintained and, as you drive in and get out of your car with your bags and baggage, you are suddenly swept up in the enthusiastic welcome that Olive bestows on everyone. – no wonder she was the first B. & B. to win the Failte Ireland Warm Welcome Award. Before you know where you are, you are ensconced on comfortable sofas being plied with tea and apple tart while Olive talks a dime a dozen. Paddy is delightful, a gentle smiling farmer, who knows and is proud of what Olive has achieved and her enthusiasm for visitors and tourists. Olive has thought of everything for the very comfortable bedrooms with all sorts of extras like electric blankets, hairdryers, and nick nacks often lacking in hotels and some rooms have Jacuzzi baths. The Nire Valley is very popular with walkers and anglers but you can drive around, like me, if you wish!! The river Nire runs beside Glasha and fishing permits are available locally. Have a delicious dinner – maybe Rack of Comeragh Lamb or Poached Monkfish, and, if you are good, Olive and Paddy will show you the back gate, which slips out onto a little winding road where, at the foot of the hill, is one of the dinkiest old pubs I have ever been in. It is like something out of a movie – absolutely wonderful and a perfect way to end the day before strolling back up to Glasha for a wonderfully peaceful sleep in the stillness of Ballymacarbry. Come down next morning and you are in for one of the best breakfasts

in Ireland – what a spread Olive puts out – one of the best I have ever seen.  Houses like Glasha are the real hidden places of Ireland very often not found by Tourists.

| Owners | Paddy and Olive O Gorman |
| --- | --- |
| Address | Glasha ,Ballymacarbry via Clonmel, Co Waterford |
| Tel / Fax | 052 36108  /052 36108 |
| No. Of rooms | 8 |
| Price, Double: | €90-€100 |
| Single: | €50 |
| Dinner | Yes – €25-€35 -BYO wine |
| Open | All Year except Christmas |
| Credit Cards | Visa MC |
| Directions | Sign posted on Clonmel to Dungarvan road |
| Email | glasha@eircom.net |
| | www.lucindaosullivan.com/glashafarmhouse |

# richmond country house

Richmond House is the real thing – no faux Georgian facades here. Everything about it is real, classy, elegant and understated. The house, built in 1704 by the Earl of Cork and Burlington, looms tall and stately, gazing serenely out over the fields and private parkland, in the heart of the Blackwater Valley. It has been the Deevy family home for forty years or so, as Jean Deevy and her husband, Bill, a Vet, raised their six children there. To aid the restoration and upkeep of such a large house Jean started out simply doing Bed & Breakfast when en-suites were "en heard of". She provided very well cooked homely food, introducing to her repertoire the "rage of the time" the old prawn cocktail – always a winner. Times move on and Richmond House is now a place to be reckoned with for Jean's son, Paul, is a very fine Chef, having trained in the Hotel Industry, moving on then to Switzerland, before returning to take up the reins at Richmond House along with his wife, Claire. The bedrooms are gracious and spacious, furnished with antiques, and so comfortable you just want to snuggle in there and not move out. Have a drink in the old conservatory or in the butter yellow drawingroom, meet the people, who will be salivating at the thought Paul Deevy's innovative but classically French oriented food. Think Fresh Chorizo risotto with steamed mussels and a light butter sauce followed by local fillet of lamb with tapenade, sundried tomatoes and a rosemary jus … have the Crinnaughtaun apple juice at breakfast … it helps the hangover. Richmond House is the place to stay if you are in the Dungarvan West Waterford area or, better still, just make it your destination for a fabulous weekend.

| | |
|---|---|
| Owners | Paul and Clare Deevy |
| Address | Cappoquin, Co Waterford |
| Tel / Fax | 058 54278  /058 54988 |
| No. Of rooms | 9 |
| Price, Double: | From €140 |
| Single: | From €70 |
| Dinner | Yes |
| Open | January 23rd – December 23rd |
| Credit Cards | All major cards accepted |
| Directions | Take Waterford road from Cappoquin Richmond House is on the right |
| Email | info@richmondhouse.net |

www.lucindaosullivan.com/richmondhouse

# sion hill house

My beloved is convinced we only bought our house in Monkstown because, when we came to view, there was a lamb in the garden. The former owner had a sheep farm in Mayo and had brought the lamb up for his kids- to play with not to eat, I hasten to add. Mind you, he promised us one for the deep freeze and I am still waiting. I was so mesmerized by the nuzzling lamb that there was no chance of me looking for rising damp.

I fell madly in love with the whole ethos of Sion Hill House and Gardens which is in a spectacular position high up overlooking all of Waterford City and the River Suir. This is a true haven on five acres of magnificent gardens which George and Antoinette Kavanagh have carefully restored to the original layout of 250 years ago with in or around 1000 species of plants many of them

rare. Winding pathways lead to hidden groves, a walled garden and a pond with tree ferns and a Coptic monk lodged in an old garden wall. Not only that but there is lots of wildlife in the garden including a tame fox on the property who comes right up and sits beside George. Now, don't expect a command performance every day. George and Antoinette are brilliant, charming and hospitable. George is a fund of local historical knowledge and the house is full of Victoriana, ancient swords, with the odd stuffed bird of the feathered variety and stags heads here and there. Small boys and big boys will find them fascinating. The bedrooms, furnished with antiques, are lovely and airy with big comfortable beds, fine linen and T.V.'s With such a magnificent view I could not bear to pull the curtains preferring instead to watch the boats alternately chugging out or gliding in. The Tall Ships are coming to Waterford in July 2005 and this is the House to book because you will certainly be in the front row of the Dress Circle.

| | |
|---|---|
| Owners | George & Antoinette Kavanagh |
| Address | Ferrybank ,Waterford City |
| Tel / Fax | 051 851558  /051 851678 |
| No. Of rooms | 4 |
| Price, Double: | €80-€110 |
| Single: | |
| Family | €100-160 |
| Dinner | No |
| Open | January 5th – December 20th |
| Credit Cards | Visa MC |
| Directions | From Waterford take Rosslare Route N25 on left beside Ard Ri Hotel. |
| Email | sionhill@eircom.net |

www.lucindaosullivan.com/sionhillhouse

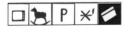

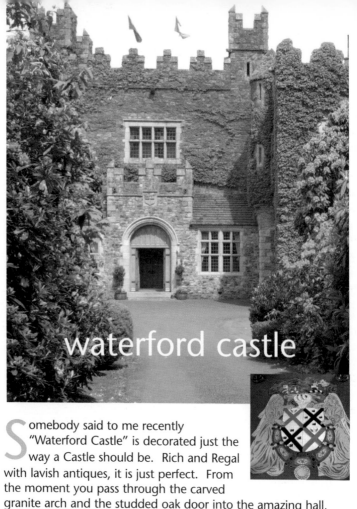

# waterford castle

Somebody said to me recently "Waterford Castle" is decorated just the way a Castle should be. Rich and Regal with lavish antiques, it is just perfect. From the moment you pass through the carved granite arch and the studded oak door into the amazing hall, dominated by a beautiful French style cavernous fireplace, and absorb the magnificent tapestries, from generations of yore, hanging on all sides, you are in another world. You will notice on the chimneybreast, raised proud from the stone, like some giant ornate jewel, the carved Fitzgerald coat of arms, and likewise the crested carpet on the floor, for Waterford Castle, built in the 15th Century, and the Norman Keep before that, were in the hands of the Fitzgerald family for 800 years. Fabulously located on its own private 310 acre island on the River Suir, yet just 2 miles out of the hustle and bustle of Waterford City, the Castle is surrounded by woodlands and an 18 hole Championship Golf Course. How do we get to the island I can hear you ask? You just nip out the Dunmore East Road, turn left at the sign and head down to the private ferry which transports you across the little channel into another world of luxurious retreat, sanctuary and seclusion. Over a thousand years ago the first inhabitants cut a rough track to their secure settlement but this is now a tree lined driveway lush with ever changing colours and ahead stands the stunning Castle picturesque and enchanting. The splendid 19 bedrooms are bright and airy with magnificent views of the surrounding estate and guests get the feeling, for this is the way they are received, that they are residents rather than mere "hotel guests". Dinner in the Munster Dining Room with its original oak panelled walls and ornate ceilings is an experience and a memorable occasion. The Chefs will tempt you with perhaps Kebab of Dublin Bay Prawns with Roast Garlic, Basil and Cherry tomatoes followed by such delicious goodies as Moroccan Spiced Fillet of Aged Beef with a Cous Cous Salad and a Pepper Salsa Verde. It really is an island dream and a very romantic place.

The tasteful detail of the interior reflects the olde world charm of a 15th century Castle. The guestrooms and suites are particularly spacious and well appointed with stunning views of the surrounding estate and golf course. All private and public rooms have been individually decorated and the elegance of the original features have been preserved within the Castle. Beautiful antique furniture, original oak panelling, ornate original plaster ceilings and a Elizabethan Stone fireplace complement the Castle.

| | |
|---|---|
| Owners | Waterford Castle Hotel & Golf Club |
| Address | The Island, Ballinakill, Waterford. |
| | Tel  051 878203 Fax 051 879316 |
| No. Of rooms | 19 |
| Price, Double: | €195-€485 |
| Single: | €180-€260 |
| Dinner | Restaurant |
| Open | Open all year save 24/25/26 Dec |
| | and 3rd Jan –5th Feb. |
| Credit Cards | Visa, MC, Diners, Amex |
| Directions | Look for sign to left off Dunmore |
| | East Road |
| Email | info@waterfordcastle.com |

www.lucindaosullivan.com/waterfordcastle

# county wexford

The Vikings have a lot to answer for when you think of the number of Irish Towns they have founded. Wexford in the southeast, the sunniest part of the Country, is another example of their handiwork. It's very narrow streets are now teeming with thriving shops and businesses and, along the quayside, on the Slaney estuary stands a statue to Commadore John Barry, the Wexford man who founded the U.S. Navy during their War of Independence. This lively town is host to the ever popular and important Wexford Opera Festival every year. South of the town, almost on the extreme southeast corner of the country is Rosslare Strand with its magnificent beach and two 18 hole golf courses. Rosslare Strand is very popular with Irish people but very often missed by tourists who disembark from the ferry at

"People are wrong when the say opera is not what it used to be.
It is what it used to be.
That is what is wrong with it."

(Noel Coward)

Rosslare Harbour and drive madly out of the area. Going north
the county has many towns with historic connections and none
more so than Enniscorthy. Enjoy its period atmosphere and its
connection with the 1798 Rebellion with its backdrop of Vinegar
Hill site of a famous battle of the same name. Also worth seeing is
the Pugin designed St. Aidan's Cathedral. Of more recent interest
are the sandy beaches at Curracloe where Steven Speilberg shot
those realistic battle scenes for his movie "Saving Private Ryan".
In the south west of the county, on the banks of the Barrow
Estuary in the quaint village of Arthurstown close to Dunbrody
Abbey and less than a mile from Ballyhack from whence the ferry
runs to Passage East in County Waterford.

# ferrycarrig hotel

The Ferrycarrig Hotel is set low down by the Slaney Estuary just outside Wexford town and is a wonderful places to stay for all ages, families, couples, just everyone, for it is lively and friendly, providing good food, and all facilities for the perfect fun relaxing break.

My relationship with the Ferrycarrig got off to a rocky start because I arrived, anonymously of course, to review Tides, their fine dining Restaurant to discover it was closed that night. It was before their smart new makeover and in my review I described the high windowed corridors as Prague 1963 and made reference to their lift, which dropped six inches before it took off upwards. I have to say they took it on the chin magnificently and with a considerable sense of humour invited me back some months later to officially declare open the new lift! None of those idiosyncrasies will be found now in the completely renovated Ferrycarrig 2004 – in fact I rather miss the little lift. All of the bedrooms now are large and spacious with cool modern East Coast American style décor – very smart- and some have balconies. The casual buzzy 120-seat Boat House Restaurant provides super food for adults and children with the seasonal menu rotating on a three-night basis to avoid repetition if you are staying for a few nights. Tides, which provides excellent gourmet food, doesn't open every night so do check if it is there you are particularly interested in. It's an interesting Hotel to walk around from the big Moroccan style resident's lounge to the tucked away little area off the bar. There is an excellent leisure centre and very well supervised pool and this is a real place for everyone to enjoy. The General Manager, Mark Browne, is absolutely charming and will ensure you enjoy your stay.

| Owners | Mark Browne (General Manager) |
|--------|-------------------------------|
| Address | Ferrycarrig Bridge ,Wexford |
| Tel / Fax | 053 20999  /053 20982 |

| | |
|--|--|
| No. Of rooms | 102 |
| Price, Double: | €150-€300 |
| Single: | Single Supplement applies |
| Dinner | Yes – 2 Restaurants |
| Open | All Year |
| Credit Cards | Visa Mc Diners Amex |
| Directions | On N 11 2 miles north of Wexford town |

Email
res.ferrycarrig@ferrycarrighotel.com
www.lucindaosullivan.com/ferrycarrighotel

# glendine country house

## ARTHURSTOWN AND BALLYHACK

From whichever side you approach Arthurstown and Ballyhack on the Hook peninsula, there is a positive feel of never neverland. Coming from either Dublin or from Rosslare, the Duncannon roundabout outside Wexford is where you change worlds. Sit back and head straight out towards Ballyhack, trundling through hedgerows, along miles of straight road downward towards the sea, taking you little by little back into history to this totally undeveloped area. From the Waterford side you take the ferry at Passage East, it only takes a few minutes but the scene is set, and as you approach Ballyhack and its 16th Century Castle you are almost exhilarated. Drive a short distance to Arthurstown and pull up at the dinky little pub, the King's Bay Inn, on the left, have a pint of the black stuff, you deserve it after that five-minute voyage!

## GLENDINE COUNTRY HOUSE

Tom and Ann Crosbie's fine Georgian Country House sits on 50 acres of beautifully landscaped gardens and paddocks, which hold their Highland cows, Jacob sheep, and deer. A Dower house to the Dunbrody Estate it was first occupied by the Chichester family and later by land agents until one of them absconded with the Nursery Nurse causing a great scandal. Glendine retains many of its original 1830 features and, overlooking the Barrow Estuary, all of the rooms have sea views. Beautifully decorated, using subtle historic Farrow & Ball colours, the large en suite bedrooms have Victorian beds, pitch pine floors, crisp cotton sheets, original

wooden shutters, but also have the comforts of T.V. hairdryers and clock radios for when you get tired of looking at the sea, if that is possible. The lovely yellow drawingroom with fine fireplace, antiques and works of art, is comfortable and welcoming. Breakfasts are hearty and wholesome, using organic produce where possible. Help yourself to a fine range of fresh fruits, cereals, porridge, yoghurts and juices followed by delicious cooked breakfast with lashings of wholemeal toast or homemade brown bread. Two cosy 4 Star Self-catering cottages are available in the courtyard, converted from the original 1830 stone buildings and these sleep five people comfortably. Dinner is not available at Glendine but soup and open brown bread sandwiches are happily provided at all times. There are very nice Restaurants close by and excellent pub grub. Glendine has a wine licence but you can also bring your own. It is a lovely place to stay in a superb location and Tosh and Annie are charming hosts.

| | |
|---|---|
| Owners | Tom & Ann Crosbie |
| Address | Arthurstown ,Co Wexford |
| Tel / Fax | 051 389500 /051 389677 |
| No. Of rooms | 10 |
| Price, Double:/Twin | €100 Enquire re rates for 2 self catering cottages |
| Dinner | No |
| Open | All year except Christmas |
| Credit Cards | Visa MC ,Diners |
| Directions | From New Ross turn right at The Brandon House Hotel, Pass J.F Kennedy Arboretum, Arthurstown is signposted |
| Email | glendinehouse@eircom.net www.lucindaosullivan.com/glendinecountryhouse |

# kelly's resort hotel

Since 1895 four successive generations of the Kelly family have each added their own stamp to Kelly's Resort Hotel. Bill Kelly and his wife Isabelle have, in turn, enlarged and added a whole new cool modern dimension in the last few years. Being right on the beach there is that up market sandy resort ethos and atmosphere for, as soon as you swish up and park you will see people strolling around in their bathrobes between Leisure and Beauty Centre, Hairdressers, pools or hot tub – it is just switch off time. I know people who drive down to Kelly's, park their car, and don't move it again until they are leaving. Why would they, everything one wants is encompassed within the Hotel. When one mentions Kelly's Hotel people generally say – "oh – the food is fabulous and one eats so much". That's true. Its like a cruise ship, non-stop wonderful food all included in your rate. Breakfast and lunch are available buffet style in the Ivy Room or with formal service in the beautiful Beaches Restaurant which had €1m spent on it alone last year. Dinner is a formal affair in Beaches followed by dancing each evening. Kelly's Irish Art Collection is famed and each year too you see new works hanging. Isabelle's family is in the wine business in the Chateauneuf-du-Pape region of France and most of the Hotel's wines are imported directly, offering tremendous quality at very affordable prices. Bedrooms are lovely – some with doors opening out onto your own mini terrace or else have balconies. As well as Beaches there is also the La Marine Restaurant (not included in the "all in" rate) and Bar which is very popular with visitors to Rosslare. Throughout the year

there are different breaks Cookery or Wine weeks, Antiques, Gardening, Ballroom Dancing and Golf Clinics. Kelly's mainly operates on an all inclusive package, anything from two days to a week, and for what is included offer superb value. Sometimes, midweek only, they do a room and breakfast rate if that is what you want, and you can

dine in either Beaches or La Marine. Just when you thought everything was already available at Kelly's they have a new surprise for their guests – a fabulous new Destination Spa is opening in July 2004.

| | |
|---|---|
| Owners | Bill Kelly |
| Address | Rosslare Strand, Co. Wexford. |
| Tel / Fax | 053 32114 / 053 32222 |
| No. Of rooms | 118 |
| Price, Double/Twin | €130 - €170 + 10% Service Charge |
| Single: | €70 - €80 + 10% Service Charge All Inclusive Rates from €230 pps for 2 days upwards. |
| Dinner | 2 Restaurants |
| Open | 27th February – 12th December |
| Credit Cards | Visa. M.C. Amex |
| Directions | On Rosslare Strand |
| Email | kellyhot@iol.ie |

www.lucindaosullivan.com/kellyshotel

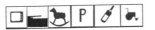

monfin house

Have you been to Monfin? I asked my Bank Manager, a Wexford man, as indeed was his Assistant who was from nearby Gorey. "No", they both replied. You must go there I said to them – not together you understand … it's wonderful and soon with my book everyone will know all about it. Monfin is a glorious Georgian House just outside Enniscorthy built in 1823 which Chris and Avril Stewart, who bought the house three or four years ago, have painstakingly restored, bringing it up to speed in terms of luxury and comfort, with elegant classic décor without compromising the ethos of the house. There are four beautiful double bedrooms, two with mahogany four-poster beds and two with spa baths. Dinner – five courses – (24 hour notice please) is available in the beautiful red diningroom and you can be assured of the best and most interesting of wines as Chris's day job is in the Wine business. Dinner might include a ragout of seafood, followed by Rack of Lamb with a thyme jus but, do discuss on booking in case you are allergic to anything, as it is a no choice menu. Chris and Avril also host themed evenings, or one or two night breaks with French, Italian or rather interestingly Indonesian food involving wine tasting on the Friday, followed by a superb dinner on the Saturday (4/6 people). Breakfast at Monfin is excellent starting with freshly squeezed juices, Wexford summer fruits, winter compotes, homemade cereals and breads followed by the hot variety. Monfin House is a super place for a few days away to relax

and enjoy the good things of life and
do visit St. Aidan's cathedral in
Enniscorthy designed by the famous
Architect Pugin.

| | |
|---|---|
| Owners | Avril and Chris Stewart |
| Address | St Johns, Enniscorthy, Co Wexford |
| Tel / Fax | 054 38582  /054 38583 |
| No. Of rooms | 4 |
| Price, Double: | €130-€150 |
| Single: | €85 |
| Dinner | Yes |
| Open | February -November |
| Credit Cards | All major cards accepted |
| Directions | Take New Ross road out of Eniscorthy  Turn left after Mill _ mile on right hand side |
| Email | info@monfinhouse.com |

www.lucindaosullivan.com/monfinhouse

# county wicklow

Truly the Garden of Ireland County Wicklow is rich in mountains, valleys, gorse, heather, and bracken, and as any hiker, cyclist and motorist will undoubtedly agree, it more than deserves its title. Less than an hour's drive from Dublin City, the county quickly portrays the two dominant traditions in Irish history, Glendalough with its Monastic background and the magnificent Anglo Irish Powerscourt Estate at Enniskerry. Glendalough set in a remote valley is a mediaeval Monastic site with its period cemetery, round tower, remains of a monastic chapel and its two lakes, is a very popular haunt for tourists. The area is surrounded by a number of pleasant welcoming villages, Knockree, Roundwood, Laragh, Rathdrum and, of course, Avoca whose name was made famous by the poet Thomas Moore, and the peaceful village of Aughrim. Enniskerry in the foothills of the Wicklow Mountains is a very popular summer weekend destination for tourists, who trudge uphill from buses to the Powerscourt Estate and its beautiful gardens. Powerscourt also boasts two 18-hole golf courses. The impressive Powerscourt House designed by Richard Cassels was destroyed by fire in 1974, it has now been restored to house a number of shops and a restaurant. The famous Powerscourt Waterfall is almost three miles away from the main house but is still within the Estate's extensive grounds. On the coast to the south is Greystones a pretty somnambulant town where many of the inhabitants commute to Dublin daily and is close to the town in Ireland with the longest name, Newtownmountkennedy, and the famous Druid's Glen Golf Course. Further south is Wicklow town, which enjoys a fine setting on the coast, and proudly proclaims its restored historic jail. On south past the beautiful sandy beach at Brittas Bay brings you to Arklow town a chiefly commercial centre well known as a boat building and fishing port and immortalized by Van Morrison in his "Streets of Arklow".

"It takes a lot of experience for a girl to kiss like a beginner."
(*Ladies Home Journal*, 1948)

# ballyknocken country house

A friend of mine said to me "I had the holiday of my life" at Ballyknocken and that, in fact, was in Catherine Fulvio's mother's day for she ran the house as a Farmhouse B & B before the days of "en-suites" so, as they say in Ireland, "Catherine didn't lick it off the ground" for she learnt at her mother's knee the fine art of hospitality. The diminutive dynamo Catherine then pursued a career at the top end of the Hospitality industry for some years. Having married her Italian husband, Claudio, she returned in 1999 to Ballyknocken to take over the reins where she is now wowing the critics with her superb cooking and beautifully upgraded 4 Star Country House. Catherine sources the best of ingredients from country markets and local butchers and is an imaginative, superb, Ballymaloe trained cook. The bedrooms are beautifully furnished in a light period style with Victorian baths and also have T.V. Breakfast is a lavish buffet with a choice of hot food from the full Irish to smoked salmon potato cakes. Ballyknocken is ideal for romantic breaks or, just any break, and for those who like walking holidays, for which special packages are available. If you want to be independent there is the self-catering 2 bedroomed Milking Parlour Loft Apartment with splendid views over Glenealy Valley and Carrick Forest. You can also be "semi-self-catering" as, for a supplement, you can have breakfast or dinner at the main house as you so wish. This year Ballyknocken Cookery School has opened so there are all sorts of weekend and short break cookery classes. Catherine can organize anything – picnics are available – flowers, champagne in the room for that special weekend – just ask and it will be done. Being in the Garden of Ireland yet so close to Dublin makes Ballyknocken a wonderful place for a break at any time of year – it's a Happy House.

| | |
|---|---|
| Owners | Catherine Fulvio |
| Address | Glenealy, Ashford ,Co Wicklow |
| Tel / Fax | 0404 44627 /0404 44696 |
| No. Of rooms | 7 |
| Price, Double: | €99 - €110 |
| Single: | €69 |
| Dinner | Yes except Sunday and Bank Holiday Mondays |
| Open | Mid January –Mid December |
| Credit Cards | Visa /MC |
| Directions | From Dublin take N11 to Ashford village Turn right at Texaco Station continue for 3 miles house on right |

Email
cfulvio@ballyknocken.com
www.lucindaosullivan.com/ballyknockenhouse

# clone house

t was a milestone birthday in my Better Half's life. Such a special and intimate occasion that must be celebrated by a big bash in a local Hotel or, worse still, a surprise party. As the event loomed large he threatened family and friends that if they foisted any of the aforementioned events on us, he would not feign surprise, hug everyone in view or shed the compulsory tears when the children would thrust the bouquet of carnations. Instead he would flee the party and emigrate the following day to a remote island for ever more. When they handed us an envelope (not brown) we thought maybe the one way tickets to the remote island was enclosed but it was much better, it was a ticket to four days of total bliss at Clone House near Aughrim, Co. Wicklow, the Garden of Ireland.

Italian born Carla Watson and her American husband Jeff, have done a superb job on Clone House, deep in the Wicklow Hills yet only 15 minutes from the sea, with a lavish makeover resulting in quite splendid bedrooms and a totally splendid house. Just over an hour from Dublin we found Clone House without any great difficulty but it is wise to contact Carla by phone as she will, with the expertise of an Air Traffic Controller, guide you in. For me she represented St. Peter at the gates of Heaven when the great doors of Clone House were swung open by this ball of energy, yet an angelic and nymph like creature. Carla led us up the steps of that Regal Staircase to our boudoir, which was absolutely gorgeous. A huge big comfortable canopied bed, piled high with cushions and

feather filled pillows and bolster was placed at an angle in the room to take full advantage of the sun streaming through casting its rays on all the beautifully chosen and polished antiques. Dinner was great fun and here too is another special thing about Clone - the cuisine is Tuscan - reflecting Carla's origins - and also incorporating organic produce from her garden – White truffle risotto and Quail wrapped in Parma Ham- were two of the starters we had during our stay after which we lingered each night in the tiny snug at the back of the house with another jorum and making new friends. I fooled myself in the mornings in the sauna that I was losing stones and then rapidly undid it again eating memorable foccacia with pitted olives and Feta washed down with thimbles of white port in the garden in the afternoon. That is the way to live – can I say more? Yes, I can, Clone thankfully is a strictly non smoking house. Great food, Great people, Great fun.

| Owners | Carla Edigati Watson |
| Address | Aughrim,Co Wicklow ,Ireland |
| Tel / Fax | 0402 36121  /0402 36029 |
| No. Of rooms | 7 |
| Price, Double: | €140-€180 |
| Single: | €110-€180 |
| Dinner | Yes |
| Open | All Year |
| Credit Cards | Visa MC Diners |
| Directions | Follow house signs from Aughrim or Woodenbridge |
| Email | stay@clonsehouse.com |

www.lucindaosullivan.com/clonehouse

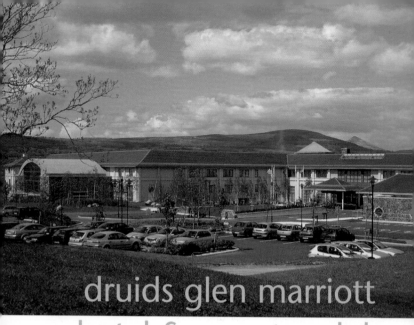

# druids glen marriott
## hotel & country club

I thought I had lost him, he thought he had died and gone to Heaven, for the Druids Glen Marriott Hotel & Country Club on a 400 acre estate, has not just one, but two Championship Golf Courses. We could have stayed there forever and just met up for dinner in the evenings because, while he was on the Golf Course, I was indulging myself in the magnificent Spa. 18 metre swimming pool, whirlpool, solarium, steam room, aroma steam and hydrotherapy rooms and a fitness suite (not me!!) over looking the pool area. I was more interested in the luxurious massages and beauty treatments. Druids Glen Hotel is the first Marriott hotel in Ireland, and is open just two years, whilst Druids Glen Golf Course has been host to four Irish opens from 1996-1999 and in April 2002 hosted the prestigious Seve Trophy Golf Tournament. There is also a Golf Academy and a large practice area. There are lots of other activities locally – quad biking, horse riding, and, of course, you are smack between the Wicklow Mountains and the Sea – the world is your oyster.  Druid,s Glen is perfect for a visit to Dublin where husband doesn't want to trail around the shops – you can take off with the credit card and he will have plenty to occupy him.  You don't even have to go to Town for there is great shopping in Blackrock, Glasthule and Bray.  The bedrooms are an enormous 37 square metres with minibars, room safes, T.V. data port, and ironing boards. There are interconnecting family rooms or you can have two under 16's share your room free of charge

and there are
also rooms
adapted for disabled guests. Two
Restaurants from which to choose, the
specialist American style Flynn's Steakhouse and the larger Druids
Restaurant in which breakfast, lunch and dinner are served. Druids
Glen is also perfect for Corporate groups.

| | |
|---|---|
| Owners | B.J. Schreuder – General Manager |
| Address | Newtownmountkennedy, Co. Wicklow. |
| Tel / Fax | 01 2870800/ 01 2870801 |
| No. Of rooms | 148 |
| Price, Double King | From €150 - €230 |
| Double Double | Up to 2 Children under age 16 share parent's room free. |
| | Family Interconnecting Rooms Also. |
| Dinner | 2 Restaurants |
| Open | All Year |
| Credit Cards | All Major Cards |
| Directions | 20 miles south of Dublin on N.11 look for signs. |
| Email | mhrs.dubgs.reservations@marriotthotels.com |
| | www.lucindaosullivan.com/druidsglen |

# houses in alphabetical order

# slow down

Enjoying Ireland is not about tearing down a motorway at 90 miles an hour, for doing it that way you will miss the whole ethos of the country. Tourists planning their trip in advance from America and other distant places tend to look at our little green, bear shaped, island in the Atlantic on the edge of Europe and think "we'll see it all in 3 days" – believe me you won't have even "done" West Cork properly in that time. You may have seen the views but you won't have experienced anything except a sore backside from sitting in the driving seat!

Take time out, get to know your hosts, it makes such a difference. They can give you all the local lore and recommendations. Go down to the local pub – you won't be long on your own – because the Irish love to talk. Every time I arrive at a destination, my first stop is the nearest hairdressers, which absolutely delights Brendan, for he then has an hour to find the best pub and in no time at all, the locals will have found out his seed, breed and generation, and he will have been rewarded with the best local information.

In the immortal words of Simon and Garfunkel - "Slow Down You Move to Fast..."

Quality, luxury and style

# MEET

# THE

# FAMILY

In 1885 John Francis Brown planted his first vines in Milawa, Australia. It was the beginning of a great dynasty - the Brown Family and their wines. Today, three generations of the Brown family are involved in producing the most varied and fascinating wines in Australia. They are brought to you in Ireland exlusively by Woodford Bourne. Isn't it time you let us introduce you to the wonderful Brown Brothers?

*Woodford Bourne is a Member of the DCC PLC Group*

e Ltd, 79 Broomhill Road, Tallaght, Dublin 24, Ireland. Ph: +353 1 4047300  Fx: +353 1 4047311  e: wine@woodfordbourne.com  www.woodfordbourne.com

Notes

## Notes

Notes

Notes

Notes

Notes

## Notes